4.95

JOHNSON
ROBERT E. LEE THE CHRISTIAN

Printed in the United States of America

BOOKS BY WILLIAM J. JOHNSON

ROBERT E. LEE THE CHRISTIAN
GEORGE WASHINGTON THE CHRISTIAN
ABRAHAM LINCOLN THE CHRISTIAN

ROBERT E. LEE THE CHRISTIAN

WILLIAM J. JOHNSON

BOX 236, MILFORD, MI. 48042

Cover design by Myron Quinton
Cover © copyright 1976 Mott Media

TO MY SIX GRANDSONS

F. JACKSON HAUSER
LINCOLN A. HAUSER
WILLIAM WASHINGTON HILLMAN
CHARLES VAN KIRK HILLMAN
DONALD EDISON HILLMAN
MALCOLM EVERETT HILLMAN

IN THE

HOPE THAT THEY MAY BE LIKE

ROBERT E. LEE

IN

PURITY AND NOBILITY OF CHARACTER

"The law of his God is in his heart; none of his steps shall slide." —*Psalm 37. 31.*

CONTENTS

CHAPTER		PAGE
	Foreword	13
I.	Christian Lineage	21
II.	Home Training	26
III.	Model Youth and Young Man	30
IV.	A Model Soldier	34
V.	Revered and Loved	42
VI.	A Christian on the Frontier	48
VII.	The Great Decision	60
VIII.	God's Will	75
IX.	The Soul of Lee	83
X.	God His Helper	106
XI.	The Heart of Lee	113
XII.	Sabbath Observance	126
XIII.	Unselfish Nobleness	131
XIV.	A Kneeling Christian	140
XV.	Great in Defeat	150
XVI.	A Christian College President	159
XVII.	The College Chapel	167
XVIII.	Religious Welfare of Students	176
XIX.	Financial Temptation	186
XX.	The Comforter	192
XXI.	General Lee and Temperance	200
XXII.	A Man of Prayer	205
XXIII.	An Active Churchman	212
XXIV.	General Lee and the Bible	217
XXV.	The Sunset	225

CONTENTS

CHAPTER		PAGE
XXVI.	Testimony of Associates	234
XXVII.	Tributes	245
XXVIII.	His Crowning Grace	250
	Sources of Information	255
	Where Found	261
	Names of the Deity	275
	Notes	278
	Lee Memorial Chapel	279
	Abraham Lincoln Was a Lee	280
	Index	283

FOREWORD

IN the southern Indiana home of my favorite uncle, whose honored name I bear, there hung a picture of the radiant face from which shone the magnanimous soul of ROBERT E. LEE. As a lad I stood before it often and long, lured, not by the military uniform with brass buttons, but by the look of gentleness and kindness. There was formed between us an enduring spiritual friendship. An indelible picture was stamped upon my mind, which is undimmed to this day.

Eighteen years ago, while gathering material in the Library of Congress for my book on *George Washington the Christian*, I became interested in the religious life of Robert E. Lee. Mrs. Johnstone and I went to Richmond and Lexington, Virginia, to visit the places intimately associated with him. It was then that I resolved that some day I would write a book on ROBERT E. LEE THE CHRISTIAN.

"Rhetoric should not usurp the place of history. Truth, simply told, is better than oratory."

There is a tendency to exalt unduly the

virtues of great men, and to magnify the religious character of one professing to be a Christian. Some may doubt the genuineness of a man's piety, fearing that his profession of religion was merely nominal. Incidents, letters, "orders" of the army, etc., will show beyond a doubt that, with General Lee, vital godliness was a reality.

"No picture of Robert E. Lee could be complete that did not portray the religious side of his character. It was the basis upon which all else rested. It was the source of his strength, the law of his life, the guide for his every act, and the support upon which he leaned in every trial."

His confidential letters to members of his family reflect his Christian faith.

"Naturally, without effort, without obtrusiveness or ostentation, his never-failing trust in God and submission to His will shines out in his intimate letters to the members of his family. Neither victory nor defeat deflects his soul from its constant look upward to the Almighty disposer of events."

It has been noted "how little of war and how much of Christian feeling and domestic affection" his home letters contain.[1]

"His correspondence reveals him as a man who lived in the presence of God; who looked to God continually for guidance and strength; whose mind and heart were saturated with faith and trust in God.[2]

"Those who knew General Lee in private could not fail to remark that religion was with him something more than an empty name; that it was a power lodged in the heart and controlling his whole nature."

In his public papers, written during the war, he never failed, whenever opportunity offered, to call the attention of the people to the great Disposer of all human events and to inspire them with gratitude or submission, as the circumstances might suggest. Even in a brief telegraphic dispatch, he rarely fails to make mention of the Sovereign Ruler of all.

When General Lee won a victory, he gave the glory to a higher Power. A firm believer in an overruling Providence, his "dispatches," "reports," and "orders" gratefully recognized "the Lord of Hosts" as the "Giver of victory," and breathed a spirit of trust in and humble dependence upon Him. Throughout the war almost every military dispatch or private letter written by him contained some allusion to his trust and confidence in God.

Pages could be filled with quotations from General Lee's "orders" and "dispatches," expressing profound "gratitude to Almighty

God"; his "thanks to God"; his "gratitude to Him who hath given us the victory"; his sense of "the blessing of Almighty God"; his "grateful thanks to the only Giver of victory"; and his "ascribing unto the Lord of Hosts the glory due His name."

"No one can familiarize himself with Lee's life without seeing that he was a man consecrated to the work of his Divine Master, and amid all conditions possessed a mind stayed on Him."

"He constantly felt, and in every proper way acknowledged, his utter dependence upon God's overruling providence."

"A prisoner of war on parole"—his application for "amnesty" never granted; his beautiful Arlington home, bequeathed to his wife by the adopted son of George Washington, confiscated by the Federal government; the Washington family relics taken from Arlington, retained by the government; disfranchised—the commonest privileges of citizenship, to vote or hold office, accorded the most ignorant of freed slaves, "who could neither write nor understand its laws, and to aliens who could not speak its language," but denied to General Lee—he bowed beneath the weight of the cross and labored earnestly to accomplish what he wrote in a letter:

FOREWORD

I THINK IT WISEST NOT TO KEEP OPEN THE SORES OF WAR BUT TO FOLLOW THE EXAMPLE OF THOSE NATIONS WHO ENDEAVORED TO OBLITERATE THE MARKS OF CIVIL STRIFE AND TO COMMIT TO OBLIVION THE FEELINGS IT ENGENDERED.

Colonel Charles Cornwallis Chesney, a distinguished British military critic, said of Lee:

"The day will come when the evil passions of the great civil strife will sleep in oblivion and North and South do justice to each other's motives and forget each other's wrongs. Then history will speak with clear voice of the deeds done on either side, and the citizens of the whole Union do justice to the memories of the dead.

"In strategy mighty, in battle terrible, in adversity as in prosperity a hero indeed, with the simple devotion to duty and the rare purity of a Christian knight, he joined all the kingly qualities of a leader of men."[3]

In this book, the chronological order has been followed, that we may see how constantly and continuously he was guided and sustained, throughout his whole life, by Divine Grace and Wisdom. Lee's age and the date of the events on that page are given at the bottom of the page. Quotations from Lee, except very short ones, are in smaller type, without quotation marks.

After years of study of the life and character of Robert Edward Lee, I fail to find, in his whole career, from the cradle to the grave, a flaw in his relations to his family, his friends, his associates, or his enemies; in his conduct at home, in school, in the field, in the college, or in the church; and in his moral, social, and religious character.

The Rev. R. A. Holland, in a memorial address at the Kentucky Military Institute shortly after General Lee's death, exclaims:

"Behold in him a character which, if not perfect, conceals its faults with the effulgence of its virtues, even as the sun conceals the spots on its dazzling disk."

Since the days when "Enoch walked with God"; since the days when "Abraham was called the Friend of God"; since the days when the Son of man taught that "Whosoever will save his life shall lose it: and whosoever will lose his life for my sake shall find it"; since the days when the evangelist John was known as "that disciple whom Jesus loved"; since the days when the apostle Paul declared that he "was not disobedient unto the heavenly vision," no great historic personage blazes with a greater luster of purity, nobility, and lofty Christian manhood throughout his whole life, than ROBERT E. LEE.

Merriam Park,
Saint Paul, Minnesota.

W. J. Johnson

CHAPTER I

CHRISTIAN LINEAGE

THE LEES

SUCH a character as ROBERT E. LEE does not happen—it is the product of generations of Christian ancestry. It is not an individual accomplishment—it is a family development.

Of pure Norman blood, the long and illustrious line of the Lees may be traced back to Launcelot Lee, who accompanied William the Conqueror and his sixty thousand knights—the flower and chivalry of Normandy—upon his conquest of the English throne, and was rewarded for his services by an estate in Essex, 1066 A. D. For seven hundred years the name of Lee occurs continually in English history, and, we are told, "always in honorable mention."[4]

One of his paternal ancestors, Lionel Lee, raised a company of gentlemen and marched with Richard Coeur de Lion on his third crusade to the Holy Land in 1192, and "for his gallantry at Acre, and in other battles with the infidel, was, on his return home, made the first Earl of Litchfield, and presented by the king with the estate of Ditchley; subsequently held, as all the readers of Walter Scott must remember, by that indomitable old knight, Sir Henry Lee, who figures so conspicuously in *Woodstock*."[5]

Two other Lees "so distinguished themselves as to have their banners suspended in Saint George's Chapel, Windsor, with the Lee coat-of-arms emblazoned thereon."[6]

The founder of the family in America was Richard Lee, great-great-grandfather of Robert E. Lee, who came from England to Virginia. That he was a man of high character, and of notable piety for an age of free living and worldly tendencies, his will shows. In that document he bequeaths his soul "to that good and gracious God that gave it to me, and to my blessed Redeemer, Jesus Christ, assuredly trusting, in and by His meritorious death and Passion, to receive salvation."[7]

The Carters

Lee's mother was Anne Hill Carter. "a daughter of the family of Carter, long distinguished in the Virginia colony for the munificent application of large wealth to purposes of charity, learning, and religion."[8]

His great-great-grandfather was Robert Carter. A large stone which in former times stood at the east end of Christ Church in Lancaster County, Virginia, bore record that he was

"An honorable man, who by noble endowments and pure morals gave luster to his gentle birth. . . . Possessed of ample wealth, blamelessly acquired, he built and endowed at his own expense this sacred edifice—a signal monument of his piety toward God. He furnished it richly."[9]

Among the papers of Lee's mother, the wife of Major-General Henry Lee, and the daughter of Charles Carter, was found the following obituary testimonial:

"In fulfilling the duties of his station, he proved himself to be an Israelite indeed, in whom there was no guile."[10]

His Father

Lee's father was the celebrated cavalry leader of the Revolution, Major-General Henry Lee, popularly known as "Light Horse Harry," the personal and political friend of Washington, who summed up his career, "First in war, first in peace, first in the hearts of his countrymen."

Move to Alexandria

Robert Edward was born on Monday, January 19, 1807, at Stratford, on the Potomac,

1807]   [Birth

Westmoreland County, Virginia, the same county in which George Washington was born seventy-five years before. When he was four years old [1811], the family moved to Alexandria, Virginia, "the better to educate the children." When he was six years old [1813], his father went to the West Indies, hoping to restore his health after an injury, remained there five years, and died on Monday, March 15, 1818, on the return journey, at the home of General Nathanael Greene, on Cumberland Island, Georgia, which had been presented to him by the state of Georgia for services rendered her in the Revolution. General Henry Lee was buried there.

"What Is Happiness?"

Writing from Nassau, West Indies, Sunday, February 9, 1817, to Robert's oldest brother, Charles Carter Lee, a student at Harvard University, the father said:

"My dear Carter, what is happiness? . . . Peace of mind based on piety to Almighty God, unconscious innocence of conduct, with good will to man; health of body, health of mind, with prosperity in our vocation; a sweet, affectionate wife; . . . children devoted to truth, honor, right, and duty, with love and respect to their parents; and faithful and warm-hearted friends, in a country politically and religiously free—this is my definition."[11]

Robert Always Good

In this letter, the father asks about the different children. Of Robert, ten years old, he said: "Robert was always good, and will be confirmed in his happy turn of mind by his ever-watchful and affectionate mother. Does he strengthen his native tendency?"[12]

This is the earliest statement known about Lee's character.

1817] [Age 10

CHAPTER II

HOME TRAINING

His Mother

ROBERT was eleven years old when his father died. Since he was six years old his training had devolved upon his devoted mother, gentle and pious, with a sincere and simple faith in God's providence. She "appears to have been a woman of high character and to have taught her son practical as well as moral excellence." She "was a communicant of Christ Church, Alexandria, Virginia; and her children were taught the Episcopal catechism by young William Meade, eventually Bishop of Virginia."[13] Robert was born, baptized, and reared in the Episcopal Church. In a letter written March 7, 1866, he said that Bishop Meade "had known me in childhood, when I recited to him the church catechism, taught me by my mother before I could read."[14]

"The molding hand of the mother was giving shape to that moral character which stands yet in our annals unrivaled for earnestness and self-sacrifice."[15]

She watched over his daily life and "planted

him in the soil of truth, morality, and religion, so that his boyhood was marked by everything that produces nobility of character in manhood."[16]

"Her prayers with her tender admonition were the forces that cast his growing character in that mold of noble self-control that made the child the father of the man."[17]

"At his mother's knee, that divinely appointed school whose instruction no other teacher can impart, and whose lessons when faithfully given are worth all others we receive, he learned his obligations to his Maker and his fellow man."[18]

From her he learned to "practice self-denial and self-control, as well as the strictest economy in all financial concerns," virtues which he retained throughout life.[19]

"It was from her lips he learned the Bible, from her teaching he drank in the sincere belief in revealed religion which he never lost. It was she who imbued her great son with an ineradicable belief in the efficacy of prayer, and in the reality of God's interposition in everyday affairs of the true believer."[20]

In later life, in almost the very words of Abraham Lincoln, he said, "All I am I owe to my mother." Lincoln said, "All that I am or hope to be, I owe to my aged mother."

The Boy

From persons who knew him as a boy, "we are assured that Lee's childhood was as remarkable as his manhood for the modesty and thoughtfulness of his character and for the performance of every duty which devolved upon him."[21]

He worshiped in old Christ Church, Alexandria, Virginia, in the same church in which Washington had been a pewholder.

Many a Christmas, with the other boys of the neighborhood, he brought the evergreen and helped to decorate the church.[22]

Devotion to Mother

Lee's mother was a great invalid; one of his sisters, Anne, was delicate, and for many years was absent in Philadelphia, under the care of physicians. The oldest son, Charles Carter, was at Cambridge (Harvard University); Sydney Smith, the other son, was in the navy; the other sister, Mildred, was too young to be of much help in household matters. So Robert was the housekeeper, carried the keys, attended to the marketing, managed all of the outdoor business, and took care of his mother's horses.

At the hour when the other schoolboys went to play, he hurried home to order his mother's drive and would be seen carrying her in his arms to the carriage and arranged her cushions with the gentleness of an experienced nurse.[23] He was careful to fasten the curtains and close up the cracks with newspapers to keep draughts from her and used his powers to entertain and divert her.

"He waited on her, nursed her when sick, drove with her, obeyed her every wish; and this reciprocal love was a goodly picture in old Alexandria to those who saw mother and son in those days."[24]

More than one of his cousins have recorded that what impressed them most in their youth was "Robert's devotion to his mother." That devotion may be imagined from his mother's words when he was about to leave for West Point Military Academy:

"How," she exclaimed to a friend, in an uncontrolled burst of emotion, "can I ever live without him? He has been son, daughter, protector—he has been all in all to me!"[25]

CHAPTER III

MODEL YOUTH AND YOUNG MAN

HABITS

HE never drank intoxicating liquor, never used tobacco, or indulged in any of the petty vices to which youth is apt.[26]

Said one of the family: "The other boys used to drink from the glasses of the gentlemen; but Robert never would join them. He was different."[27]

A near relative wrote after his death, "I knew Robert Lee from the time I can first recollect, and I never remember hearing him censured for anything in my life."[28]

ALEXANDRIA ACADEMY

"No breach of discipline nor any neglect of duty was ever charged against him during his years of study in the Alexandria Academy. No unbecoming word ever fell from his lips; but speech and action indicated always that he lived as under his great Taskmaster's eye."[29] December 15, 1866, from Lexington, Virginia, General Lee wrote a letter to his old teacher, Mr. W. B. Leary, in which he said, "I pray that the evening of your days may be blessed with peace and tranquillity, and that a merciful God may guide and protect you to the end." [30]

For special preparation to enter West Point Military Academy, in the winter of 1824-25, he attended the school of Mr. Benjamin Hallowell, a Quaker, for many years a famous teacher in Alexandria. He says: "He was a most exemplary student in every respect. He was never behind time at his studies; never failed in a single recitation; was perfectly observant of the rules and regulations of the institution; was gentlemanly, unobtrusive, and respectful in all his deportment to teachers and his fellow students."[31]

INFLUENCE OF YOUNG MAN'S LIFE

One of Lee's friends gives a remarkable incident to show the influence which, even at this early day (1825), his simple dignity and high sense of right exercised upon all who came in contact with him, the old as well as the young. Being invited, during a vacation, to visit a friend of his family who lived in the gay, rollicking style then but too common in old Virginia, he found in his host one of the grand old gentlemen of that day, with every fascination of mind and manner, who, though not of dissipated habits, led a life which the sterner sense of the boy could not approve. The old man shrunk before the unspoken rebuke of the youthful hero. Coming to the boy's bedside the night before his departure, he lamented the idle and useless life into which he had fallen, excusing himself upon the score of loneliness and the sorrow which weighed upon him in the loss of those most dear. In the most impressive manner he besought his young guest to be warned by his example; prayed him to cherish the good habits he had already acquired, and promised to listen to his entreaties that he would change his own life, and thereby secure more entirely his respect and affection.[32]

At West Point

In 1825, when he was eighteen, Lee entered West Point Military Academy. Here "he avoided tobacco and intoxicating liquors, used no profane or immoral language."[33]

It is said that during his four years at West Point he never received a reprimand or a demerit.[34]

"Throughout his whole student life he performed no act which his pious mother could not have fully approved."[35]

"His unquestioned temperance and self-control in moral matters appear doubly creditable when we read the statements made by

MODEL YOUTH AND YOUNG MAN 33

Colonel Thayer, superintendent of West Point at that time, to President John Quincy Adams, as to the drunkenness and dissipation generally prevalent among the young men."[36]

Lee graduated in 1829, being twenty-two years old.

CHAPTER IV

A MODEL SOLDIER

Death of Mother

THE first duty to which Lieutenant Lee was assigned was in the Engineer Corps at Fortress Monroe, in 1829. Soon after arrival there he was summoned to "Ravensworth," a great estate in Fairfax County, Virginia, about ten miles from Arlington, where his mother lay dying. He cared for her tenderly and was her constant nurse. "He mixed every dose of medicine she took and was with her night and day. If he left the room, she kept her eye on the door till he returned. He never left her but for a short time,"[37] until the end came.

Marriage

Thursday evening, June 30, 1831, at the age of twenty-four, at Arlington, Virginia, Lieutenant Robert E. Lee was married to Mary Randolph Custis, aged twenty-three, the great-granddaughter of Mrs. Washington. Her father, George Washington Parke Custis, was the grandson of Mrs. Washington, and the adopted son of George Washington. Nellie

A MODEL SOLDIER

Custis was her aunt. The marriage ceremony was performed by the Rev. Dr. Reuel Keith, of the Episcopal Theological Seminary, near Alexandria, Virginia.

CAREFUL IN CONVERSATION

Mr. James Eveleth, who was a clerk in the Engineer Department at Fortress Monroe, while Lieutenant Robert E. Lee was stationed there from 1829 to 1834, said:

"There never was a man more universally beloved and respected. He never uttered a word among his most intimate associates that might not have been spoken in the presence of the most refined woman. It can always be said of him that he was never heard to speak disparagingly of anyone, and where anyone was heard so to speak in his presence, he would always recall some trait of excellence in the absent one."[38]

"BEAU-IDEAL OF A CHRISTIAN"

Gen. Montgomery C. Meigs, who was assistant to Lieutenant Lee in some engineering work on the Mississippi at Saint Louis, Missouri, in 1837, said, "He was a model of a soldier and the beau-ideal of a Christian."[39]

IN HIS FATHER'S FOOTSTEPS

General Lee told an interesting little incident

connected with his oldest boy, George Washington Custis, which we will give here.

When a very little child, his father took him to walk in the snow one winter's day, at Arlington, holding him by the hand. Soon the boy dropped behind. Looking over his shoulder, Lee saw Custis imitating his every movement, with head and shoulders erect, putting his feet exactly in his father's footprints. "When I saw this," said the General, "I said to myself, 'It behooves me to walk very straight, when this fellow is already following in my tracks.'" And, accordingly, there was never a more circumspect father than was this great man.[40]

Lee was promoted to first lieutenant in 1836.

Letter to His Wife

In a letter to his wife at Arlington, Virginia, Monday, October 16, 1837, written from Saint Louis, Missouri, he said, "I pray God to watch over and direct our efforts in guarding our dear little son that we may bring him up in the way he should go."[41]

He was made a captain in 1838.

"Pussyism"

General Henry J. Hunt, who participated in the Mexican War, tells the following:

A MODEL SOLDIER

"In 1843-44 I was stationed at Fort Hamilton, New York Harbor. General Lee was the engineer officer in charge of the works there, and I saw much of him. He was then about thirty-five years of age, as fine-looking a man as one would wish to see, of perfect figure and strikingly handsome. Quiet and dignified in manner, of cheerful disposition, always pleasant and considerate, he seemed to me the perfect type of *a gentleman*. His family, then with him, consisted of Mrs. Lee, their little daughter, Mary, and the two boys, Custis and 'Rooney' [W. H. F.]. They formed a charming portion of our little society. Lee was a vestryman of the little parish church of Fort Hamilton, of which the post chaplain was the rector, and as thorough in the discharge of his church as of other duties.

"But the Tractarian movement had reached America; Tract No. XC had been published. Puseyism was a bone of contention. The excitement invaded our little parish, and it created feeling, for the 'Low Church' members vehemently suspected the rector of 'High Church' views, because of certain suspicious prayers that he used to which they had not been accustomed. From all this Captain Lee kept aloof, and, as he was altogether too important a member to make his views a matter of indifference, various were the efforts made to draw him out—each party hoping for his powerful support—but without success, for he always contrived in some pleasant way to avoid any expression of opinion that would commit him to either faction.

"One evening he came into the quarters of one of us youngsters, where a number of officers and one or two of the neighbors were assembled. Soon the inevitable subject came up and was discussed with considerable warmth, and, on the parts of two or three, with some feeling. Captain Lee was quiet, but, to those who understood him, evidently amused at the efforts to draw him out. On some direct attempt to do so, he turned to me and in his impressive, grave manner, said:

I am glad to see that you keep aloof from the dispute that is disturbing our little parish. That is right, and we must not get mixed up in it; we must support each other in that. But I must give you some advice about it, in order that we may understand each other: *Beware of Pussyism! Pussyism* is always bad, and may lead to unchristian feeling; therefore, beware of *Pussyism!*

"The ludicrous turn given by his pronunciation, and its aptness to the feeling that one or two had displayed, ended the matter in a general burst of laughter, for the manner more than the words conveyed his meaning. It became rather a joke at my expense, however, for sometimes when several of us met, he would look at me in a grave way, shake his head, and say, 'Keep clear of this Pussyism!' And that was as near as they ever got to committing Captain Lee to a church quarrel."[42]

"Learn to Be Good"

In a letter to his second son, William H. Fitzhugh Lee, nine years old, from Fort Hamilton, New York, Tuesday, March 31, 1846, Lee said:

You and Custis must take great care of your kind mother and dear sisters when your father is dead. To do that you must learn to be good. Be true, kind and generous, and pray earnestly to God to enable you to "keep His commandments, and walk in the same all the days of your life."[43]

"My Dear Boys"

A year later, Saturday, February 27, 1847, on a boat sailing to Mexico, he wrote a long letter to "My dear Boys"—Custis was fourteen and Fitzhugh ten—in which he said:

I shall not feel my long separation from you, if I find that my absence has been of no injury to you, and that you have both grown in goodness and knowledge, as well as stature. But, ah! how much

I will suffer on my return, if the reverse has occurred! You enter all my thoughts, into all my prayers; and on you, in part, will depend whether I shall be happy or miserable, as you know how much I love you. You must do all in your power to save me pain.

The letter closed with, "Be sure I am thinking of you, and that you have the prayers of your affectionate father."[44]

Attends Episcopal Service

In a private letter, Sunday, April 25, 1847, while in the Mexican War, he said:

This morning I attended the Episcopal service within the fort [the fort of Perote]. It was held on the parade. The minister was a Mr. McCarty, the chaplain of the Second Brigade, First Division. Many officers and soldiers were grouped around. I endeavored to give thanks to our Heavenly Father for all His mercies to me, for His preservation of me through all the dangers I have passed, and all the blessings which He has bestowed upon me, for I know I fall far short of my obligations. . . .

We must trust to an overruling Providence, by whom we will be governed for the best, and to our own resources.[45]

Loves a Joke

In a letter to a lady cousin, dated City of Mexico, Wednesday, April 12, 1848, Lee said:

A MODEL SOLDIER

It seems that all in Alexandria are progressing as usual, and that nothing will stop their marrying and being given in marriage. Tell Miss —— she had better dismiss that young divine and marry a soldier. There is some chance of the latter being shot, but it requires a particular dispensation of Providence to rid her of the former.[46]

Thankfulness to God

A letter to his brother, Captain Sydney Smith Lee, United States Navy, dated at Arlington, Friday, June 30, 1848, telling of his home-coming after an absence of two years in the Mexican War, closed, "I have much cause for thankfulness and gratitude to that good God who has once more united us."[47]

In 1848 he was made a colonel.

CHAPTER V

REVERED AND LOVED

"Everybody Loves Colonel Lee"

In 1849, Lee moved to Baltimore, Maryland, where he lived three years. He attended Saint Peter's Episcopal Church, the rector being the Rev. Dr. Thomas Atkinson. His son, Captain Robert E. Lee, Jr., tells of hearing two ladies who were visiting the Lees say, "Everybody and everything—his family, his friends, his horse, his dog—loves Colonel Lee."[48]

Children's Companion

Captain Robert E. Lee, Jr., his youngest son, tells of early impressions of his father:

"From that early time I began to be impressed with my father's character, as compared with other men. Every member of the household respected, revered, and loved him as a matter of course, but it began to dawn on me that everyone else with whom I was thrown held him high in their regard. At forty-five years of age he was active, strong, and as handsome as he had ever been. He was always bright and gay with us little folk, romping, playing, and joking with us. With the older children he was just as companionable, and I have seen him join my elder brothers and their friends when they would try their powers at a high jump put up in our yard. The two younger children he petted a great deal, and our greatest treat was to get into his bed in the morning and lie close to him, listening while he talked to us in his bright, entertaining way. This custom was kept up until we were ten years old and over. Although he was so joyous and familiar with us, he was very firm on all proper occasions, never indulged us in anything that was not good for us, and exacted the most implicit obedience. I always knew that it was impossible to disobey my father. I felt it in me, I never thought why, but was perfectly sure when he gave an order that it had to be obeyed."[49]

Counsel to His Son

In a letter to his oldest son, George Washington Custis Lee, who was at West Point, written from Baltimore, Sunday, May 4, 1851, Lee counseled him: "Hold yourself above every mean action. Be strictly honorable in every act, and be not ashamed to do right. Acknowledge right to be your aim and strive to reach it."[50]

In another letter to Custis, written from his home at Arlington, Sunday, December 28, 1851, he said:

May you have many happy years, all bringing you an increase of virtue and wisdom, all witnessing your prosperity in this life, all bringing you nearer to everlasting happiness hereafter. May God in His great mercy grant me this, my constant prayer.[51]

Frankness and Duty

General Lee exemplified in his own life in the highest degree the advice he gave in the following letter to his oldest son, Custis, written from Arlington, Monday, April 5, 1852:

Your letters breathe a true spirit of frankness; they have given myself and your mother great pleasure. You must study to be frank with the world. Frankness is the child of honesty and courage. . . . Never do a wrong thing to make a friend or to keep one. . . . Above all, do not appear to others what you are not. . . .

In regard to duty, let me, in conclusion of this hasty letter, inform you that nearly a hundred years ago there was a day of remarkable darkness and gloom, still known as the Dark Day—a day when the light of the sun was slowly extinguished, as if by an eclipse. The legislature of Connecticut was in session, and as its members saw the unexpected and unaccountable darkness coming on, they shared the general awe and terror. It was supposed

REVERED AND LOVED

by many that the last day—the Day of Judgment—had come. Someone in consternation of the hour moved an adjournment. Then there arose an old Pilgrim legislator, Davenport, of Stamford, and said that if the last day had come he desired to be found at his place doing his duty, and, therefore, moved that candles be brought in so that the House could proceed with its business. There was a quietness in that man's mind, the quietness of heavenly wisdom and inflexible willingness to obey present duty.

Duty, then, is the sublimest word in our language. Do your duty in all things, like the old Puritan. You cannot do more; you should never wish to do less. Never let me or your mother wear one gray hair for lack of duty on your part.[52]

Superintendent of West Point

Lee was appointed superintendent of West Point Military Academy in 1852 and remained there three years.

Punctual

His youngest son, Captain Robert E. Lee, Jr., says of his father, when superintendent of the United States Military Academy at West Point:

"My father was the most punctual man I ever knew. He was always ready for family prayers, and at all meal times, and met every engagement, business or social, on the moment. He expected all of us to be the same and impressed upon us the necessity of forming such habits, for the convenience of all concerned. I never knew him late for the Sunday service at the post chapel. He appeared in uniform some minutes before anyone else, and would jokingly rally my mother and sisters for being late, or forgetting something at the last moment. When he could wait no longer, he would say, 'Well, I am off,' and march away to church by himself, or with any of us who might be ready. Then he took his seat, well up in the middle aisle; and I remember he got always very drowsy during the sermon, and sometimes caught a little nap. At that time this drowsiness of my father's seemed something awful to me. I knew it was very hard for me to keep awake, and frequently did not; but why he, who I believed could do everything that was right, without an effort, should sometimes be overcome, I could not understand, and did not try to do so."[53]

Death of Mrs. Lee's Mother

Mrs. Lee's mother (Mrs. G. W. P. Custis) died at Arlington in the spring of 1853.

In a letter to his wife soon after this sad event, Colonel Lee said:

May God give you strength to enable you to bear and say, "His will be done." She has gone from all trouble, care, and sorrow to a holy immortality, there to rejoice and praise forever the God and Saviour she so long and truly served. Let that be our comfort and that our consolation. May our death be like hers, and may we meet in happiness in heaven.[54]

1853] [Age 46

CHAPTER VI

A CHRISTIAN ON THE FRONTIER

BECOMES MEMBER OF CHURCH

"He did not become a member of the church (Protestant Episcopal) until shortly after his return from Mexico; but his regular attendance upon its services and the singular rectitude of his conduct leave no doubt that he was seeking amid those temptations of ambition and pleasure, which assailed his opening manhood, to make the divine canon his supreme law, and to mold his character in accordance with that comprehensive precept of apostolic wisdom: 'Whatsoever things are true, whatsoever things are honest, whatsoever things are just, whatsoever things are pure, whatsoever things are lovely, whatsoever things are of good report; if there be any virtue, and if there be any praise, think on these things' (Philippians 4. 8)."[55]

In the summer of 1853 he was confirmed by Bishop John Johns, of Virginia, in Christ Church, Alexandria, Virginia. After the service, Bishop Johns said to him, "If you will be as faithful a soldier of the cross as you have been of your country, the church will be proud

A CHRISTIAN ON THE FRONTIER 49

of you, and when your warfare is over, I shall covet your crown."[56]

The vow thus taken "was never forgotten nor disregarded until in the silence of a dying-chamber his upward-pointing finger revealed the soul's hope and expectation of reward."[57]

In his earlier years he seems to have had some speculative doubts. One of his devout biographers says:

"Although at that time, and for a score of years thereafter, his estimate of his own unworthiness, and some mistaken views of Christ, perhaps, prevented his making an avowal of the Christian faith and becoming a communicant of the church, he was nevertheless all the while guided and restrained by belief in the Bible, reverence for its Author as revealed therein, reliance *more or less* implicit upon the Saviour, and prayer secret, but sincere."[58]

All his children were baptized at Arlington by their pastor, the Rev. Charles B. Dana, the rector of Christ Church, Alexandria, Virginia.[59]

GOES TO TEXAS

In 1855 he was made a lieutenant-colonel in the regular army and entered upon his new duties. In 1855-57 he was stationed in Texas.

The family went to Arlington, in 1855, to

live in the home of Mrs. Lee's father, George Washington Parke Custis.

Death of Youngest Sister

Monday, August 11, 1856, Lee wrote to his wife from Camp Cooper, Texas, regarding the death of his youngest sister, Mrs. Edward Vernon Childe, in Paris, France:

I pray that her life has but just begun, and I trust that our merciful God only so suddenly and earnestly snatched her away because He then saw that it was the fittest moment to take her to Himself. May a pure and eternal life now be hers; and may we all live so that when we die it may be open to us.[60]

In the Hands of God

From Camp Cooper, Monday, September 1, 1856, he replied to a letter from his wife, informing him that his name was frequently mentioned for a brigadier-generalcy:

We are all in the hands of a kind God, who will do for us what is best, and more than we deserve, and we have only to endeavor to deserve more, and to do our duty to Him ourselves. May we all deserve His mercy, His care, and protection.[61]

Views on Slavery

In a letter to his wife from Camp Brown, Texas, Saturday, December 27, 1856, Lee gave in graphic words his views on slavery:

I believe, in this enlightened age, there are few who will not acknowledge that slavery as an institution is a moral and political evil. It is idle to expatiate on its disadvantages. I think it is a greater evil to the white than to the colored race. While my feelings are strongly enlisted in behalf of the latter, my sympathies are more deeply for the former. The blacks are immeasurably better off here than in Africa morally, socially, and physically. The painful discipline they are undergoing is necessary for their instruction as a race, and, I hope, will prepare and lead them to better things. How long their subjection may be necessary is known and ordered by a wise and merciful Providence. Their emancipation will sooner result from a mild and melting influence than the storms and contests of fiery controversy. This influence, though slow, is sure.

The doctrines and miracles of our Saviour have required nearly two thousand years to convert but a small part of the human race, and even among Christian nations what gross errors still exist! While we see the course of the final abolition of slavery is onward, and we give it the aid of our prayers, and all justifiable means in our power, we must leave the progress as well as the result in His hands who sees the end and who chooses to work by slow things, and with whom a thousand years are as a single day; although the abolitionist must know this, and must see that he has neither the right nor the power of operating except by moral

52   ROBERT E. LEE THE CHRISTIAN

means and suasion; and if he means well to the slave, he must not create angry feelings in the matter. That although he may not approve the mode by which it pleases Providence to accomplish His purposes, the result will never be the same; that the reasons he gives for interference in what he has no concern hold good for every kind of interference with our neighbors when we disapprove their conduct. Is it not strange that the descendants of those Pilgrim Fathers who crossed the Atlantic to preserve the freedom of their opinion have always proved themselves intolerant of the spiritual liberty of others?[62]

Christmas, 1856

In the same letter, telling how he spent Christmas, he said: "After dispensing my presents, I went to church; the discourse was on the birth of our Saviour. It was not as simply or touchingly told as in the Bible."[63]

Letter to Sick Wife

Having heard that Mrs. Lee was sick, he wrote to her from Fort Brown, Texas, Wednesday, January 7, 1857, "I pray and trust your efforts and the prayers of those who love you may be favorably answered."[64]

Easter Service in His Tent

Sunday, April 5, 1857, from Fort Mason,

A CHRISTIAN ON THE FRONTIER 53

Texas, en route to his old camp at Camp Cooper, Easter Sunday, Lee wrote to his wife:

This is Easter Sunday. I hope you have been able to attend the services at church. My own have been performed alone in my tent, I hope with a humble, grateful, and penitent heart, and will be acceptable to our Heavenly Father. May He continue His mercies to us both and all our children, relatives, and friends, and in His own good time unite us in worship, if not on earth, forever in heaven.[65]

Sustained by Divine Providence

Sunday, April 19, 1857, from Camp Cooper, he wrote to his wife again:

After an absence of over seven months I have returned to my Texas home. I heard of Indians on the way but saw none. I feel always as safe in the wilderness as in the crowded city. I know in whose powerful hands I am, and on Him I rely and feel that in all our life we are upheld and sustained by Divine Providence, and that Providence requires us to use the means He has put under our control. He designs no blessing to idle and inactive wishes, and the only miracle He now exhibits to us is the power He gives to Truth and Justice to work their way in this wicked world.[66]

Performs Burial Service

In a letter to his wife, dated Tuesday, June

9, 1857, from Camp Cooper, Lee told of the sickness of the troops, and said:

A bright little boy died a few days since. He was the only child, and his parents were much affected by his loss. They expressed a desire to have him buried with Christian rites, and asked me to perform the ceremony; so for the first time in my life I read the beautiful funeral service of our church [Episcopal] over the grave to a large and attentive audience of soldiers.[67]

Another Funeral Service

In a later letter, dated Monday, June 22, 1857, he told of the death of another little boy, the son of one of the sergeants. He said:

Last Thursday the little waxen form was committed to the earth. His father came to me, tears flowing down his cheeks, and asked me to read the funeral service over his body, which I did at the grave for the second time in my life. I hope I shall not be called on again, for though I believe that it is far better for the child to be called by its Heavenly Creator into His presence in its purity and innocence, unpolluted by sin, and uncontaminated by the vices of the world, still it so wrings a parent's heart with anguish that it is painful to see. Yet I know it was done in mercy to both—mercy to the child, mercy to the parents. The former has been saved from sin and misery here, and the latter have been given a touching and powerful inducement to

A CHRISTIAN ON THE FRONTIER

prepare for hereafter. May it prove effectual and may they require no further severe admonition!

May God guard and bless you all.[68]

Death of Mrs. Lee's Father

Mrs. Lee's father, George Washington Parke Custis, the grandson of Mrs. Washington, and the last survivor of the household of Mount Vernon, died on Saturday, October 10, 1857, in his seventy-sixth year. Colonel Lee obtained a leave of absence from his Texas post and returned east in order to finish settling his father-in-law's estate, of which he had been named executor in the will.

Capture of John Brown

"During this visit he was selected by the secretary of war to suppress the famous 'John Brown Raid' and was sent to Harper's Ferry in command of the United States troops." Brown was captured and handed over to the proper civil authorities. Afterward Lee remarked to Mrs. Pickett's father, "I am glad we did not have to kill him, for I believe he is an honest, conscientious old man."[69]

Lee remained at Arlington, his home, until early in 1860.

The Home of Lee

General Lee was unusually happy in his

home life, and his tender devotion to his wife and children is an inspiration. One of his biographers says:

"Should we seek through all the annals of time for an illustration of the best that exists in family life, we need not go further to find the perfection and refinement of elegance and of purity than that stately mansion, the home of Lee, which from the wooded heights of Arlington looks down upon the city of Washington."[70]

Chaplain J. William Jones says, "These family letters show that a happier home circle could not be found than that of this loving family, when the storm of war burst upon the peaceful abode of Arlington."[71]

Letter to His Son Fitzhugh

Sunday, May 30, 1858, Lee wrote from Arlington, to his second son, W. H. F. Lee (Fitzhugh, nicknamed "Roon"), who had joined his command as second-lieutenant, to which he had been appointed, saying:

I hope you will always be distinguished for avoidance of the "universal balm," whisky, and every immorality. Nor need you fear to be ruled out of the society that indulges in it, for you will rather acquire their esteem and respect, as all venerate, if they do not practice, virtue.

A CHRISTIAN ON THE FRONTIER

The letter closed:

May Almighty God have you in His holy keeping. To His merciful providence I commit you and will rely upon Him and the efficacy of the prayers that will be daily and hourly offered up by those who love you.[72]

Purity and Virtue

Under date of Saturday, January 1, 1859, from Arlington, he wrote to Fitzhugh, in the army in the West:

I cannot express the gratification I felt in meeting Colonel May, in New York, at the encomiums he passed upon your soldiership, zeal, and devotion to your duty. But I was more pleased at the report of your conduct. That went nearer my heart, and was of infinite comfort to me. Hold on to your purity and virtue. They will proudly sustain you in all trials and difficulties, and cheer you in every calamity.

I was sorry to see, from your letter to your mother, that you smoke occasionally. It is dangerous to meddle with. You have in store so much better employment for your mouth. Reserve it, Roon, for its legitimate pleasure. Do not poison or corrupt it with stale vapors or tarnish your beard with their stench.[73]

Again to His Son Fitzhugh

Monday, May 30, 1859, he wrote Fitzhugh, and said: "I have no enjoyment in life now

58 ROBERT E. LEE THE CHRISTIAN

but what I derive from my children. May God guard and bless them all is my constant prayer."[74]

In February, 1860, Lee was ordered to take command of the Department of Texas.

Would Not Do What Is Wrong

Friday, December 14, 1860, he wrote from San Antonio, Texas, to his son Custis at Arlington:

He [General Scruggs] thinks the Union will be dissolved in six weeks. . . . I hope, however, the wisdom and patriotism of the country will devise some way of saving it, and that a kind Providence has not yet turned the current of His blessings from us. . . . While I wish to do what is right, I am unwilling to do what is wrong, either at the bidding of the South or the North. One of their plans seems to be the renewal of the slave trade. That I am opposed to on every ground.[75]

Helps Build Church

The summer months of 1860 were spent in San Antonio. While there Lee interested himself with the good people of that town in building an Episcopal church, to which he contributed largely.[76]

Life of Washington

From Fort Mason, Wednesday, January 23, 1861, he wrote to Mrs. Lee, saying:

A CHRISTIAN ON THE FRONTIER 59

I received Everett's *Life of Washington* which you sent me and enjoyed its perusal. How his spirit would be grieved could he see the wreck of his mighty labors! I will not, however, permit myself to believe, till all the ground for hope is gone, that the work of his noble deeds will be destroyed, and that his precious advice and virtuous example will soon be forgotten by his countrymen. As far as I can judge from the papers, we are between a state of anarchy and civil war. May God avert from us both! I fear mankind for years will not be sufficiently christianized to bear the absence of restraint and force.[77]

Another Letter to His Son

Wednesday, January 30, 1861, writing from Fort Mason, Texas, to his son, he said:

The country seems to be in a lamentable condition, and may have been plunged into civil war. May God rescue us from the folly of our acts, save us from selfishness, and teach us to love our neighbors as ourselves.[78]

Two weeks after this letter was written, after the secession of Texas, he received orders "to report to the commander-in-chief at Washington," and hastened to obey the summons—reaching there on the first of March, just three days before the inauguration of President Lincoln.

CHAPTER VII

THE GREAT DECISION

FACING THE ISSUE

In April, 1861, Colonel Lee was awaiting orders at Arlington. On Thursday, April 18, he had an interview with Mr. Francis P. Blair, who, with the knowledge of Lincoln and Secretary of War Cameron, unofficially, but it is said authoritatively, offered him the command of the United States Army in the field.

Immediately on leaving Mr. Blair, Lee went to General Scott and told him of the offer, and that he "could take no part in an invasion of the Southern states."[79]

THE UPPER ROOM

The Lee mansion at Arlington, Virginia, commanded a fine view of the Potomac and the Capitol beyond. In the upper chamber of this mansion, through the long night of Friday, April 19, 1861, Lee wrestled with the question, whether to retain his command in the United States Army or to resign. The scriptural injunction, "Choose ye this day whom ye will serve," rang in his ears continually.

THE GREAT DECISION

Here is Mrs. Lee's account of the way in which his decision was made:

"The night his letter of resignation was to be written, he asked to be left alone for a time, and while he paced the chamber above, and was heard frequently to fall upon his knees and engage in prayer for divine guidance, she waited and watched and prayed below. At last he came down, early in the morning of April 20, 1861, calm, collected, almost cheerful, and said:

"Well, Mary, the question is settled. Here is my letter of resignation and a letter that I have written to General Scott."[80]

His wife's words to him were: "Whichever way you go will be in the path of duty. You will think it right, and I shall be satisfied."[81]

"My husband has wept tears of blood," wrote Mrs. Lee to his old commander, General Winfield Scott.

Eighty-seven years before, in 1774, when George Washington advocated withdrawing allegiance from King George and stated that he would fight to uphold the independence of the colonies, Mrs. Lee's grandmother, Mrs. Washington, wrote, "George is right; he is always right."[82]

A month and a half later, on the other side of the Potomac, in the city of Washington, at the Willard Hotel, on the morning of inauguration day, Abraham Lincoln "said that he wished to be left alone for a short time." The family withdrew, and Lincoln, "closeted alone with his God," was heard in prayer.[83]

These two great leaders, one of the North, the other of the South, on their knees earnestly sought divine wisdom and guidance that they might know and do the right.

His Resignation

Writing to General Winfield Scott, the commander-in-chief of the United States Army, from Arlington, Saturday, April 20, 1861, Lee said:

I therefore tender my resignation, which I request you will recommend for acceptance. It would have been presented at once [referring to his interview with General Scott on April 18] but for the struggle it has cost me to separate myself from a service to which I have devoted the best years of my life and all the ability I possessed. . . . Save in the defense of my native state, I desire never again to draw my sword.[84]

His Choice

On the same day, from Arlington, he wrote a letter to his oldest sister, Mrs. Anne R. Marshall, of Baltimore, whose husband, Judge William L. Marshall, and son espoused the Union cause, in which he said:

We are now in a state of war which will yield to nothing. The whole South is in a state of revolution, into which Virginia, after a long struggle, has been drawn; and though I recognize no necessity for this state of things, and would have foreborne and pleaded to the end for redress of grievances, real or supposed, yet in my own person, I had to meet the question whether I should take part against my native state.

With all my devotion to the Union and the feeling of loyalty and duty of an American citizen, I have not been able to make up my mind to raise my hand against my relatives, my children, my home. I have, therefore, resigned my commission in the army, and save in the defense of my native state, with the sincere hope that my poor services may never be needed, I hope I may never be called on to draw my sword.

I know you will blame me; but you must think as kindly of me as you can and believe that I have endeavored to do what I thought right. To show you the feeling and struggle it has cost me, I send you a copy of my letter of resignation. I have not time for more.

May God guard and protect you and yours and shower upon you everlasting blessings, is the prayer of your devoted brother.[85]

Letter to His Brother Sydney

On the same day he wrote his second brother, Captain Sydney Smith Lee, of the United

States Navy, who, afterward, joined the Confederacy and became a commodore in the Confederate Navy, saying:

> The question which was the subject of my earnest consultation with you on the 18th instant has in my own mind been decided. After the most anxious inquiry as to the correct course for me to pursue, I concluded to resign and sent in my resignation this morning. I wished to wait till the Ordinance of Secession should be acted on by the people of Virginia; but war seems to have commenced, and I am liable at any time to be ordered on duty which I could not conscientiously perform. To save me from such a position, and to prevent the necessity of resigning under orders, I had to act at once, and before I could see you again on the subject, as I had wished. I am now a private citizen and have no other ambition than to remain at home. Save in the defense of my native state, I have no desire ever again to draw my sword.[86]

Casts Lots With Virginia

On Sunday morning, April 21, 1861, in the churchyard of Christ Church, Alexandria, Virginia, after service, "counting the agonizing cost to his state, Lee agreed to take command of the Virginia forces, seeing only too clearly the first inevitable personal sacrifice, the loss of his Arlington home."[87]

Eighty-seven years before, in this same

THE GREAT DECISION

churchyard, one Sunday morning after service, George Washington announced his decision, "that he would fight to uphold the independence of the colonies."

Takes Command of Virginia Forces

Summoned to Richmond by the Governor of Virginia, which had seceded on Wednesday, April 17, 1861, he arrived there on Monday, April 22. He never saw Arlington again.

Three days after presenting his resignation, Tuesday, April 23, 1861, he was introduced to the Virginia Convention, meeting in Richmond, and offered by them the command of the military forces of his state, to become major-general and commander-in-chief of the forces of Virginia. In accepting, he said,

Trusting to Almighty God, an approving conscience, and the aid of my fellow citizens, I will devote myself to the defense and service of my native state, in whose behalf alone would I have ever drawn my sword.[88]

Offered Command of United States Army

After the war, Lee wrote a letter from Lexington, Virginia, under date of Tuesday, February 25, 1868, to the Honorable Reverdy Johnson, United States Senate, Washington, D. C., in regard to his having been offered the

1861] [Age 54

command of the United States Army. He said:

I never intimated to anyone that I desired the command of the United States Army; nor did I ever have a conversation with but one gentleman, Mr. Francis Preston Blair, on the subject, which was at his invitation, and, as I understood, at the instance of President Lincoln.

After listening to his remarks, I declined the offer he made me, to take command of the army that was to be brought into the field; stating, as candidly and as courteously as I could, that, though opposed to secession and deprecating war, I could take no part in an invasion of the Southern states.

I went directly from the interview with Mr. Blair to the office of General Scott; told him of the proposition that had been made me, and my decision.

Upon reflection after returning to my home, I concluded that I ought no longer to retain the commission I held in the United States Army, and on the second morning thereafter I forwarded my resignation to General Scott.

At the time I hoped that peace would have been preserved; that some way would have been found to save the country from the calamities of war; and I then had no other intention than to pass the remainder of my life as a private citizen.

Two days afterward, upon the invitation of the Governor of Virginia, I repaired to Richmond, found the convention then in session had passed the ordinance withdrawing the state from the

THE GREAT DECISION

Union, and accepted the commission of commander of its forces which was tendered me.[89]

General Lee is reported to have said to Mr. Lincoln's messenger:

Mr. Blair, I look upon secession as anarchy. If I owned the four millions of slaves in the South, I would sacrifice them all to the Union—but how can I draw my sword upon Virginia, my native state?[90]

All-Compelling Sense of Duty

Lee said to General Wade Hampton, in July, 1869,

"I could have taken no other course save in dishonor; and if it were to be gone over again, I should act in precisely the same way." [91]

Concerning his decision to decline the command of the Union Army and to join his native state, it has been said,

"Since the Son of man stood on the Mount and saw all the kingdoms of the earth and the glory thereof stretching before Him and turned away from them to the agony and bloody sweat of Gethsemane, and to the cross of Calvary beyond, no follower of the meek and lowly Saviour can have undergone a more trying ordeal or met it with a more heroic spirit of sacrifice."[92]

1861]   [Age 54

His Appearance

Alexander H. Stephens, Vice-President of the newly formed Confederacy, described Lee as he appeared on this occasion:

"As he stood there, fresh and ruddy as a David from the sheepfold, in the prime of his manly beauty, and the embodiment of a line of heroic and patriotic fathers, and worthy mothers, it was thus I first saw Robert E. Lee.

"I had preconceived ideas of the rough soldier with no time for the graces of life, and by companionship almost compelled to the vices of his profession. I did not know then that he used no stimulants, was free even from the use of tobacco, and that he was absolutely stainless in his private life. I did not know then, as I do now, that he had been a model youth and young man; but I had before me the most manly and entire gentleman that I ever saw."[93]

Peace Impossible

On Thursday, April 25, 1861, Lee wrote from Richmond to his wife at Arlington, and said:

No earthly act could give me so much pleasure as to restore peace to my country. But I fear it is now out of the power of man, and in God alone must be our trust. I think our policy should be

THE GREAT DECISION

purely on the defensive—to resist aggression and allow time to allay the passions and permit Reason to resume her sway. Virginia has to-day, I understand, joined the Confederate States. Her policy will doubtless, therefore, be shaped by united counsels. I cannot say what it will be, but trust that a merciful Providence will not dash us from the height to which his smiles have raised us. . . .

May God preserve you and yours.[94]

War Inevitable

On Friday, April 26, 1861, from Richmond, he wrote to his wife about moving to some point of safety, saying:

War is inevitable, and there is no telling when it will burst around you. . . . May God bless and preserve you and have mercy upon all our people, is the constant prayer of your affectionate husband.[95]

Another Letter to His Wife

On Tuesday, April 30, 1861, he urged again that his wife "prepare all things for removal" and closed his letter, "May God preserve you all and bring peace to our distracted country."[96]

Resigned to God's Will

On Thursday, May 2, 1861, in a letter from Richmond to his wife at Arlington, he said, "We have only to be resigned to God's will

70   ROBERT E. LEE THE CHRISTIAN

and pleasure and do all we can for our protection."[97]

HONESTY

In the same letter he said:

I have just received Custis's letter [oldest son] of the 30th, inclosing the acceptance of my resignation. It is stated that it will take effect April 25. I resigned on the 20th and wished it to take effect that day. I can not consent to its running on further, and he must receive no pay, if they tender it, beyond that day, but return the whole if need be.[98]

HIS WIFE DRIVEN FROM HOME

Wednesday, May 8, 1861, Lee wrote to his wife:

I grieve at the necessity that drives you from your home. I can appreciate your feelings on the occasion and pray that you may receive comfort and strength in the difficulties that surround you. . . . Be content and resigned to God's will. . . . I send a check for five hundred dollars; it is all I have in bank. Pay the children's school expenses.[99]

URGES WIFE TO LEAVE ARLINGTON

Saturday, May 11, 1861, he wrote to his wife, still at Arlington:

You had better complete your arrangements and retire further from the scene of war. It may burst

1861]   [Age 54

THE GREAT DECISION

upon you at any time. It is sad to think of the devastation, if not ruin, it may bring upon a spot so endeared to us. But God's will be done. We must be resigned. May He guard and keep you all, is my constant prayer.[100]

Unpublished Letter

A hitherto unpublished letter written by General Lee from Richmond to his friend and pastor, the Rev. Cornelius Walker, rector of Christ Episcopal Church, Alexandria, May 2, 1861, nine days after his appointment as commander of the military and naval forces of Virginia, reveals his spiritual state:

I am extremely obliged to you for your friendly and Christian letter of the 29th, and I thank you sincerely for your kind interest in my behalf. I shall need all your good wishes and all your prayers for strength and guidance in the struggle in which we are engaged, and earnestly and humbly look for help to Him alone who can save us, and who has permitted the dire calamity of this civil fratricidal war to impend over us. If we are not worthy that it should pass from us, may He in His great mercy shield us from its dire effects and save us from the calamity our sins have produced.

Conscious of my imperfections and the little claim I have to be classed among Christians, I know the temptations and trials I shall have to go through. May God enable me to perform my duty and not suffer me to be tempted beyond my strength.[101]

A few months before, at Springfield, Illinois, Abraham Lincoln said:

"I have always regarded Peter as sincere when he said he would never deny his Lord. Yet he did deny Him. Now I think that I shall keep my word and maintain the stand I have taken; but, then, I must remember that I am liable to infirmity, and may fall."[102]

Son Decide for Himself

Monday, May 13, 1861, Lee wrote from Richmond to his wife at Arlington:

The times are indeed calamitous. The brightness of God's countenance seems turned from us, and its mercy stopped in its blissful current. It may not always be so dark, and He may in time pardon our sins and take us under His protection. Tell Custis [his son, then a lieutenant in the Engineer Corps, United States Army] he must consult his own judgment, reason, and conscience as to the course he may take. I do not wish him to be guided by my wishes or example. If I have done wrong, let him do better. The present is a momentous question which every man must settle for himself and upon principle. Our good Bishop Meade has just come in to see me. He opens the convention to-morrow, and, I understood him to say, would preach his

THE GREAT DECISION

fiftieth anniversary sermon. God bless and guard you.[103]

ATTENDS EPISCOPAL CONVENTION

Thursday, May 16, 1861, he wrote to his wife:

I witnessed the opening of the Convention [The Episcopal Convention of the Diocese of Virginia], and heard the Bishop's [Bishop Meade, of Virginia] sermon, being the fiftieth anniversary of his ministry. It was a most impressive scene, and more than once I felt the tears coming down my cheek. It was from the text, "And Pharaoh said unto Joseph, how old art thou?" It was full of humility and self-reproach.[104]

WIFE LEAVES ARLINGTON

By this time Mrs. Lee and all the family had left Arlington. She went to "Ravensworth," Virginia, where his mother died, ten miles from Arlington toward Fairfax Court House, to stay temporarily with her aunt.

Saturday, May 25, 1861, Lee wrote to his wife:

I sympathize deeply in your feelings at leaving your dear home. I have experienced them myself, and they are constantly revived. I fear we have not been grateful enough for the happiness there within our reach, and our Heavenly Father has found it necessary to deprive us of what He has given us.

I acknowledge my ingratitude, my transgressions, and my unworthiness, and submit with resignation to what He thinks proper to inflict upon me. We must trust all then to Him.

He urged her to go further south, for safety, then added:

I must now leave the matter to you and pray that God may guard you. I know and feel the discomfort of your position, but it cannot be helped, and we must bear our trials like Christians.[105]

To His Wife

In a letter to Mrs. Lee from Richmond, Sunday, June 9, 1861, he closed, "May God guard and bless you, then, and our suffering country, and enable me to perform my duty."[106]

Another Letter to His Wife

Tuesday, June 11, 1861, he wrote:

In this time of great suffering to our state and country, our private distresses we must bear with resignation, and not aggravate them by repining, trusting to a kind and merciful God to overrule them for our good.[107]

Mrs. Lee was now staying with friends at "Kinloch," in Fauquier County, Virginia.

CHAPTER VIII

GOD'S WILL

Reliance Upon God

Bishop Joseph P. B. Wilmer, of Louisiana, in a memorial address, relates a significant conversation with General Lee:

"In what temper of mind he entered this contest, I can speak with some confidence, from personal interviews with him soon after the commencement of hostilities.

"'Is it your expectation,' I asked, 'that the issue of this war will be to perpetuate the institution of slavery?'

"'The future is in the hands of Providence,' he replied, 'but if the slaves of the South were mine, I would surrender them all without a struggle to avert the war.'

"I asked him next upon what his calculations were based in so unequal a contest, and how he expected to win success; was he looking to divided counsels in the North, or to foreign interposition? His answer showed how little he was affected by the hopes and fears which agitated ordinary minds.

"'My reliance is in the help of God.'

" 'Are you sanguine of the result?' I ventured to inquire.

" 'At present I am not concerned with results. God's will ought to be our aim, and I am contented that His designs should be accomplished and not mine.' "[108]

Gambling

He endeavored, as far as possible, to repress camp vices, especially gambling. In a special "order," he says:

The general commanding is pained to learn that the vice of gambling exists and is becoming common in this army. . . . It was not supposed that a habit so pernicious and demoralizing would be found among men engaged in a cause demanding the highest virtue and purest morality in its supporters.[109]

Love for Children

No record of General Lee's Christian character would be complete without some mention of his marked fondness for children.

"On the morning of Thursday, July 4, 1861, little Henry T—— (a bright little boy of five, and an enthusiastic Confederate) went with his father to call on General Lee at his headquarters in Richmond, and to present him with a handsome copy of the Bible in four volumes.

GOD'S WILL

"One of the staff met them at the door and reported that the general was too busy to see them; but, when the great chieftain heard the prattle of the little boy, he called to his aide to admit them.

"Receiving them with great cordiality, he accepted the gift of the Bible with evident gratification, and was fondling the little boy on his knee, when the father inconsiderately asked Henry, 'What is General Lee going to do with General Scott?'

"The little fellow, who had caught some of the slang of the camp, and fully entered into the confident spirit which we all had in those early days of the war, instantly replied, 'He is going to *whip him out of his breeches!*'

"General Lee's voice and manner instantly changed, and, lifting Henry down, he stood him up between his knees, and, looking him full in the face, said, with great gravity:

My dear little boy, you should not use such expressions; war is a serious matter, and General Scott is a great and good soldier. None of us can tell what the result of this contest will be.

"A few days after this, General Lee rode out to pay a special visit to little Henry. He told him that he wished to make him some return for his present; that he was very much pleased at such a gift from a little boy, and that he could not have given him *anything* which he would have prized so highly as the Holy Bible, especially in so convenient a form. He then handed him a copy of Mr. Custis's *Recollections of George Washington*, edited by Mrs. Lee, in which he had written his own name and its presentation to Henry."[110]

Battle of Manassas

Sunday, July 21, 1861, after the battle of Manassas, Virginia, Lee wrote to his wife:

Do not grieve for the brave dead. Sorrow for those they left behind—friends, relatives, and families. The former are at rest. The latter must suffer. The battle will be repeated there in greater force. I hope God will again smile on us and strengthen our hearts and arms.[111]

It was thought best at this time to send General Lee to take command of military operations in West Virginia.

A Glorious World

Sunday, August 4, 1861, from Huntersville, West Virginia, he wrote to his wife:

I enjoyed the mountains, as I rode along. The views are magnificent—the valleys so beautiful, and the scenery so peaceful. What a glorious world

GOD'S WILL

Almighty God has given us! How thankless and ungrateful we are, and how we labor to mar His gifts!"[112]

To His Wife

Friday, August 9, 1861, from "Camp at Valley Mountain," he wrote: "May God guard and protect you all. In Him alone is our hope."[113]

Mrs. Lee was now staying at "Audley," Clarke County, Virginia, with Mrs. Lorenzo Lewis, who had just sent her six sons into the army.

To His Daughters

Thursday, August 29, 1861, writing from Valley Mountain, West Virginia, to his two daughters who were in Richmond, he closed, "God bless you, my children, and preserve you from all harm, is the constant prayer of your devoted father."[114]

Religious Tolerance

In its religious attitude the mind of Lee was eminently catholic and tolerant. A consistent member of the Protestant Episcopal Church, the traditional and historical communion of the Cavaliers, his mind was incapable of bigotry, or exclusiveness.

An application of a Jewish soldier for per-

80 ROBERT E. LEE THE CHRISTIAN

mission to attend certain ceremonies of his synagogue in Richmond was indorsed by his captain: "Disapproved. If such applications were granted, the whole army would turn Jews or Shaking Quakers." When the paper came to General Lee, he indorsed on it, "Approved," and respectfully returned it to Captain——, with the advice that he should always respect the religious views and feelings of others.[115]

Letter to Jewish Rabbi

The following letter addressed to Rabbi M. J. Michelbacher, who had requested a furlough for Jewish soldiers, that they might return to Richmond to observe the holy days appointed by the Jewish religion, illustrates his broad charity:

Headquarters, Valley Mountain,
August 29, 1861.

Rabbi M. J. Michelbacher, Preacher Hebrew Congregation, House of Love, Richmond, Virginia:

Reverend Sir: I have just received your letter of the 23d instant requesting that a furlough from the 2d to the 15th of September be granted to the soldiers of the Jewish persuasion in the Confederate States Army, that they may participate in the approaching holy service of the synagogue. It would give me great pleasure to comply with a request so earnestly urged by you, and which, I know, would

be so highly appreciated by that class of soldiers.
But the necessities of war admit of no relaxation
of the efforts requisite for its success, nor can it be
known on what day the presence of every man may
be required.

I feel assured that neither you nor any member
of the Jewish congregation would wish to jeopardize
a cause you have so much at heart by the with-
drawal even for a season of its defenders. I cannot,
therefore, grant the general furlough you desire,
but must leave it to individuals to make their own
applications to their several commanders, in the
hope that many will be able to enjoy the privilege
you seek for them. Should any be deprived of the
opportunity of offering up their prayers according to
the rites of their church, I trust that their penitence
may nevertheless be accepted by the Most High,
and their petitions answered. That your prayers
for the success and welfare of our cause may be
answered by the Great Ruler of the universe is my
ardent wish.[116]

Great Ruler of the Universe

In a letter to his son Custis, from Valley
Mountain, West Virginia, Tuesday, September
3, 1861, speaking of driving back the enemy,
he said:

Now, to drive him farther a battle must come off,
and I am anxious to begin it. Circumstances beyond human control delay it, I know for good, but

1861]   [Age 54

I hope the Great Ruler of the universe will continue to aid and prosper us and crown at last our feeble efforts with success. . . . We cannot be always successful, and reverses must come. May God give us courage, endurance, and faith to strive to the end.[117]

Son Robert Wants to Enlist

Monday, September 9, 1861, writing to his wife concerning his youngest son, Robert, now eighteen years old, who had written his father asking permission to enter the army, he said, "I pray God to bring him to a right conclusion."[118]

Ruler of Universe

Mrs. Lee was now at Hot Springs, Bath County, Virginia.

Tuesday, September 17, 1861, writing to his wife from Valley Mountain, Lee speaks of the failure to make a contemplated attack, saying:

I had taken every precaution to insure success and counted on it. But the Ruler of the universe willed otherwise and sent a storm to disconcert a well-laid plan and to destroy my hopes.[119]

CHAPTER IX

THE SOUL OF LEE

DEATH OF COLONEL WASHINGTON

In his letter of September 17, 1861, to his wife, he also speaks of the death of Colonel John Augustine Washington, great-nephew of George Washington, and Mount Vernon's last owner bearing that name. He said:

Since I had been thrown in such immediate relations with him, I had learned to appreciate him very highly. Morning and evening have I seen him on his knees praying to his Maker.

"The righteous perisheth, and no man layeth it to heart; the merciful men are taken away, none considering that the righteous are taken away from the evil to come." May God have mercy on us all![120]

AGAIN REFERS TO COLONEL WASHINGTON

Thursday, September 26, 1861, in a letter to his wife, at Hot Springs, Virginia, from Camp on Sewell's Mountain, West Virginia, he said:

I told you of the death of Colonel Washington. I grieve for his loss, though trust him to the mercy of our Heavenly Father. May He have mercy on us all. . . . My heart is always with you and my children.

May God guard and bless you all is the constant prayer of your devoted husband.[121]

Socks for Servants

General Lee was always thoughtful and considerate of all, even the humblest servants. His wife had sent him some yarn socks, which came to him as he was preparing to follow the retreating enemy. Mrs. Lee was an invalid from rheumatism, confined to a rolling chair. To help the cause with her own hands as far as she could, she was constantly occupied in knitting socks for the soldiers and induced all around her to do the same. She sent them directly to General Lee, and he always acknowledged them. Writing to her from Sewell's Mountain, October 7, 1861, he said:

Your letter of the 2nd, with the yarn socks, four pair, was handed to me when I was preparing to follow, and I could not at the time attend to either. But I have since, and as I found Perry [his black servant—had been in the dining room at Arlington] in desperate need, I bestowed a couple of pair on him, as a present from you. The others I have put in my trunk and suppose they will fall to the lot of Meredith [his cook—a servant from the "White House," Fitzhugh's home], into the state of whose hose I have not yet inquired. Should any sick

THE SOUL OF LEE 85

man require them first, he shall have them, but
Meredith will have no one near to supply him but
me, and will naturally expect that attention.[122]

General Lee now returned to Richmond as
adviser and counselor to President Davis. Before he could visit Mrs. Lee, he was sent to
South Carolina to supervise the construction of
a line of defense along the Southern coast.

LETTER TO DAUGHTER MILDRED

Writing from Charleston, South Carolina, to
his youngest daughter, Mildred, who was at
school in Winchester, Virginia, Friday, November 15, 1861, he closed, "May God guard
and protect you, my dear child, prays your
affectionate father."[123]

"MY DARLING DAUGHTERS"

Friday, November 23, 1861, writing from
Savannah, Georgia, to "My Darling Daughters," who had written him of their visit to
"Stratford," his birthplace, he said:

I wish indeed I could see you, be with you, and
never again part from you. God only can give me
that happiness. I pray for it night and day. But
my prayers, I know, are not worthy to be heard.[124]

NO SABBATH

On Sunday, December 8, 1861, from Coosawhatchie, South Carolina, he wrote to his daughter, Annie Carter Lee:

I have taken the only quiet time I have been able to find on this holy day to thank you for your letter of the 29th ultimo. One of the miseries of war is that there is no Sabbath, and the current of work and strife has no cessation. How can we be pardoned for all our offenses![125]

Christmas Family Party, 1861

From the same place, on Sunday, December 2, 1861, Lee wrote to his wife:

If Mary and Rob get to you Christmas, you will have quite a family party, especially if Fitzhugh is not obliged to leave his home and sweet wife before that time. I shall think of you all on that holy day more intensely than usual and shall pray to the great God of Heaven to shower His blessings upon you in this world, and to unite you all in His courts in the world to come. With a grateful heart I thank Him for His preservation thus far, and trust to His mercy and kindness for the future. Oh, that I were more worthy, more thankful for all He has done and continues to do for me![126]

To Wife on Christmas Day, 1861

Writing from the same place to his wife on Christmas Day, Wednesday, 1861, he said:

If we can only become sensible of our transgressions, so as to be fully penitent and forgiven, that this heavy punishment under which we labor may with justice be removed from us and the whole nation, what a gracious consummation of all that we have endured it will be![127]

To Daughter on Christmas Day, 1861

Writing to his daughter on that same Christmas Day, he sent her a little money for a Christmas present, and said:

Yet how little will it purchase! But see how God provides for our pleasure in every way. To compensate for such "trash," I send you some sweet violets that I gathered for you this morning while covered with dense white frost, whose crystals glittered in the bright sun like diamonds, and formed a brooch of rare beauty and sweetness which could not be fabricated by the expenditure of a world of money! May God guard and preserve you for me, my dear daughter!

Then, speaking of the loss of their home at Arlington, he said:

You see what a poor sinner I am, and how unworthy to possess what was given me; for that reason it has been taken away. I pray for a better spirit, and that the hearts of our enemies may be changed.[128]

Visits Father's Grave

About this time General Lee visited the grave of his father at Dungeness, on Cumberland Island, Georgia. "He went alone to the tomb, and after a few moments of silence, plucked a flower and slowly retraced his steps."[129]

Giver of All Victories

Saturday, February 8, 1862, Lee wrote to his wife from Savannah, Georgia:

I hope, however, we shall be able to stop them [the enemy], and I daily pray to the Giver of all victories to enable us to do so. . . .

I hope God will at last crown all our efforts with success. But the contest must be long and severe, and the whole country has to go through much suffering. It is necessary we should be humbled and taught to be less boastful, less selfish, and more devoted to right and justice to all the world.[130]

Fasting and Prayer

Sunday, February 23, 1862, he wrote from Savannah, Georgia:

God, I hope, will shield us and give us success. . . .

I went yesterday to church, being the day appointed for fasting and prayer. I wish I could have passed it more devoutly. The bishop [Elliott] gave a most beautiful prayer for the President, which I hope may be heard and answered. . . .

May God bless and keep you always is the constant prayer of your husband.[131]

Reverses Necessary for Correction

In a letter to his daughter, Mildred, now "sweet sixteen," Wednesday, February 26, 1862, from Savannah, Lee said:

This is a serious period, indeed, and the times look dark, but it will brighten again, and I hope a kind Providence will yet smile upon us, and give us freedom and independence.

These reverses were necessary to make us brace ourselves for the work before us. We were getting careless and confident, and required correction. You must do all you can for our dear country. Pray for the aid of our dear Father in heaven for our suffering soldiers and their distressed families. I pray day and night for you. May Almighty God guide, guard, and protect you![132]

Not Suffered Enough

Sunday, March 2, 1862, from Savannah, he wrote to his daughter Annie:

I hope you are all well, and as happy as you can be in these perilous times to our country. They look dark at present, and it is plain we have not suffered enough, labored enough, repented enough, to deserve success. But they will brighten after awhile, and I trust that a merciful God will arouse us to a sense of our danger, bless our honest efforts, and drive back our enemies to their homes. . . . May God bless you and our dear country.[133]

ROBERT E. LEE THE CHRISTIAN

General Lee was recalled to Richmond, "and was assigned on the 13th of March, under the direction of President Jefferson Davis, to the conduct of the military operations of all the armies of the Confederate States." Mrs. Lee was still at the "White House," her son Fitzhugh's place on the Pamunkey River, where Washington married the "Widow Custis," and which had been bequeathed by G. W. P. Custis to the "second son" of General Lee's marriage with his daughter.

Death of Bishop Meade

To his wife, he wrote from Richmond, Friday, March 14, 1862, "The enemy is pushing us back in all directions, and how far he will be successful depends much upon our efforts and the mercy of Providence."

He suggests that it may be best for her to change to Richmond, then concludes:

Our good and noble Bishop Meade died last night. . . . Between six and seven P. M. yesterday, he sent for me, said he wished to bid me good-by, and to give me his blessing, which he did in the most affecting manner. Called me Robert and reverted to the time I used to say the catechism to him. He invoked the blessing of God upon me and the country.[134]

A clergyman present, in describing the last

interview, states that the Bishop said to the great soldier: "God bless you! God bless you, Robert, and fit you for your high and responsible duties. I can't call you 'General,' I must call you 'Robert'; I have heard you say your catechism too often."

General Lee was deeply affected by the interview, and when he turned to leave the room, the Bishop, much exhausted, and with great emotion, took him by the hand and said: "Heaven bless you! Heaven bless you! and give you wisdom for your important and arduous duties."[135]

Son Robert Enters Army

The next day, Saturday, March 15, 1862, Lee wrote again to his wife, from Richmond, concerning his youngest son, Robert, leaving school and entering the army:

God grant it may be for his good, as He has permitted it. I must be resigned. I told him of the exemption granted by the Secretary of War to the professors and students of the university, but he expressed no desire to take advantage of it. It would be useless for him to go, if he did not improve himself, nor would I wish him to go merely for exemption. As I have done all in the matter that seems proper and right, I must now leave the rest in the hands of our merciful God.[136]

92   ROBERT E. LEE THE CHRISTIAN

June 1, 1862, General Lee took command of the Army of Northern Virginia.

ATTENDS SERVICE IN BRIGADE

Colonel Armistead Lindsay Long, military secretary to General Lee, recorded in his diary:

June 8 (1862), Sunday—"Divine service held in the different brigades of the army. General Lee attended service at one of the right-wing brigades, attended by some of his staff."[137]

BATTLE OF COLD HARBOR

Friday, June 27, 1862, reporting to President Davis the results of the battle of Cold Harbor, Virginia, Lee said, "Profoundly grateful to Almighty God for the signal victory granted to us, it is my pleasing task to announce to you the success achieved by this army to-day."[138]

LEE'S FAMILY REMOVES TO RICHMOND

After the burning of the "White House," their son Fitzhugh's place on the Pamunkey River, Virginia, by General McClellan's army in June, 1862, Mrs. Lee and her daughters occupied a rented house on Franklin Street, in Richmond, Virginia, which is now pointed out as an object of interest to the tourist.

A LOVING FATHER

Lee's youngest son, Robert, having volunteered to join the army, went to Richmond in the spring of 1862, to see his father and receive his outfit. He said: "He was just as sweet and loving to me then as in the old days. I had seen so little of him during the last six years that I stood somewhat in awe of him. I soon found, however, that I had no cause for such feeling."[139]

Aroused out of sleep, on the field after the battle of Cold Harbor, to meet his father and his staff, Robert said: "It took me a moment or two to realize what it all meant, but when I saw my father's loving eyes and smile, it became clear to me that he had ridden by to see if I was safe and to ask how I was getting along."[140]

Robert visited the family in Richmond in the summer of 1862 and saw his father, mother, and sisters. He said: "He was the same loving father to us all, as kind and thoughtful of my mother, who was an invalid, and of us, his children, as if our comfort and happiness were all he had to care for. His great victory did not elate him, as far as one could see."[141]

Seven Days' Battles

At the close of the Seven Days' battles, in a general order to the troops, Thursday, July 7, 1862, he said:

The Commanding General, profoundly grateful to the Giver of all victory for the signal success with which He has blessed our arms, tenders his warmest thanks and congratulations to the army, by whose valor such splendid results have been achieved.

In his official report, he said, "Regret that more was not accomplished gives way to gratitude to the Sovereign Ruler of the universe for the results achieved."[142]

Gratitude to Heavenly Father

Saturday, July 9, 1862, from Dobbs Farm, on the Nine Mile Road, he wrote to his wife:

I have returned to my old quarters and am filled with gratitude to our Heavenly Father for all the mercies He has extended to us. Our success has not been so great or complete as we could have desired, but God knows what is best for us.[143]

Order for Sabbath Observance

In July, 1862, Lee issued a general order to the army in which he said, "Habitually all duties except those of inspection will be suspended during Sunday, to afford troops rest and to enable them to attend religious services."[144]

Grateful to Almighty God

Writing from Jeffersonton, Virginia, August 1862] [Age 55

26, 1862, to his daughter-in-law (Fitzhugh's wife), he said regarding her husband: "I am grateful to Almighty God for preserving, guiding, and directing him in this war! Help me pray for him for the continuance of His signal favor."[145]

"Salute the Church of God"

The Rev. Thomas U. Dudley, a chaplain in Lee's army, relates the following:

"Was he a Christian? I will relate an incident as illustrative: It was in the beginning of that long, cold winter of 1862, when the battle round Richmond had been fought, and Manassas and Sharpsburg, that the army, weary of the hard campaign, was camped on those bleak hills about Winchester. An order came for a grand review—one of those sad displays we can so well remember—so sad, and yet necessary to the discipline and efficiency of the army. There were no bright trappings, nor glitter of gold; the only glitter was the fire of determination in brave men's eyes. But all would appear in their best.

"There was a chaplain who, in obedience, as he believed to his order, put on the pure white robe of his office and went to the review. Doubtless he heard the derisive laugh, the sneering remarks of those about him, but when

96   ROBERT E. LEE THE CHRISTIAN

the command he marched with passed the great chief, the officers tell us that, lifting his hat, he said: 'I salute the church of God.' The eye that was busy inspecting the accoutrements, the arms, the troops in which he trusted to do the work he had to do, could see the chaplain's robes. The commander, who sat in the immovable majesty we can remember so well, bent his uncovered head to salute the Church of the God he served."[146]

Death of Daughter Annie

Sunday, October 26, 1862, Lee wrote to his wife about the death of their daughter, Annie, nearly twenty-three years old, to whom he was especially devoted:

I cannot express the anguish I feel at the death of our sweet Annie. To know that I shall never see her again on earth, that her place in our circle, which I always hoped one day to enjoy, is forever vacant, is agonizing in the extreme. But God, in this, as in all things, has mingled mercy with the blow, in selecting that one best prepared to leave us. May you be able to join me in saying, "His will be done!" . . .

I wish I could give you comfort, but beyond our hope in the great mercy of God, and the belief that He takes her at the time and place when it is best for her to go, there is none. May the same

THE SOUL OF LEE

mercy be extended to us all, and may we be prepared for his summons.[147]

LETTER TO DAUGHTER MARY

In a letter to another daughter, Mary Custis Lee, from "Camp near Fredericksburg," Monday, November 24, 1862, he said:

The death of my dear Annie was, indeed, to me a bitter pang, but "the Lord gave, and the Lord has taken away: blessed be the name of the Lord." In the quiet hours of the night when there is nothing to lighten the full weight of my grief, I feel as if I should be overwhelmed. I have always counted, if God should spare me a few days after this Civil War was ended, that I should have her with me, but year after year my hopes go out, and I must be resigned.[148]

She died on Monday, October 20, 1862, at White Sulphur Springs, Warren County, North Carolina. At the close of the war the citizens of the county erected over her grave a handsome monument. At their request, Lee selected the following inscription for it, saying, "They are the last lines of the hymn she asked for just before her death:

'Perfect and true are all His ways
Whom heaven adores and earth obeys.'"[149]

DEATH OF GRANDDAUGHTER

From Camp Fredericksburg, Wednesday, December 10, 1862, he wrote to his son's wife (Mrs. Wm. H. Fitzhugh Lee), just the day before the opening of the battle of Fredericksburg:

I heard yesterday, my dear daughter, with the deepest sorrow, of the death of your infant. I was so grateful at her birth. I felt that she would be such a comfort to you, such a pleasure to my dear Fitzhugh, and would fill so full the void still aching in your hearts. But you have now two sweet angels [infants] in heaven. What joy there is in the thought! I can say nothing to soften the anguish you must feel, and I know you are assured of my deep and affectionate sympathy. May God give you strength to bear the affliction He has imposed and produce future joy out of your present misery, is my earnest prayer. . . . My horse is waiting at my tent door, but I could not refrain from sending these few lines to recall to you the thought and love of

Your devoted Father,
R. E. LEE.[150]

GIVER OF ALL VICTORY

A letter to General "Stonewall" Jackson on the night of the battle of Fredericksburg, December 13, 1862, closed with: "I am truly grateful to the Giver of all victory for having blessed us thus far in our terrible struggle. I pray He may continue to do so."[151]

Christmas Day, 1862

On Christmas Day, Thursday, 1862, Lee wrote from Fredericksburg, to his youngest daughter, Mildred, who was at school in North Carolina: "You must study hard, gain knowledge, and learn your duty to God and your neighbor; that is the great object of life."[152]

A letter written on the same day to his wife in Richmond gives an interesting insight into his private feelings and views regarding the great victory at Fredericksburg:

I will commence this holy day by writing to you. My heart is filled with gratitude to Almighty God for His unspeakable mercies with which He has blessed us in this day, for those He has granted us from the beginning of life, and particularly for those He has vouchsafed us during the past year. What should have become of us without His crowning help and protection? Oh, if our people would only recognize it and cease from vain self-boasting and adulation, how strong would be my belief in final success and happiness to our country! But what a cruel thing is war; to separate and destroy families and friends, and mar the purest joys and happiness God has granted us in the world; to fill our hearts with hatred instead of love for our neighbors, and to devastate the fair face of this beautiful world! I pray that, on this day when only peace and good will are preached to mankind, better thoughts may fill the hearts of our enemies and turn them to peace.[153]

Battle of Fredericksburg

After the battle of Fredericksburg, General Lee issued a congratulatory address to the army, Wednesday, December 31, 1862, beginning:

The General commanding takes this occasion to express to the officers and soldiers of the army his high appreciation of the fortitude, valor, and devotion displayed by them, which, under the blessing of Almighty God, have added the victory of Fredericksburg to their long list of triumphs. . . .

That this great result was achieved with a loss small in point of numbers only augments the admiration with which the Commanding General regards the powers of the troops and increases his gratitude to Him who hath given us the victory. . . .

The signal manifestations of Divine mercy that have distinguished the eventful and glorious campaign of the year just closing, give assurance of hope, that, under the guidance of the same Almighty hand, the coming year will be no less fruitful of events, etc.[154]

Frees His Slaves

"Lee had no illusions about slavery. He saw its evils with an eye as clear as Wendell Phillips! He set forth his views in favor of emancipation in as positive terms as Lincoln ever employed. He freed all the slaves he owned in his own right long before the war, the few that came to him by inheritance, and within a week after the Emancipation Proclamation he set free all the Negroes received by him from the Custis estate, having previous to that time made his arrangements to do so in conformity with the provisions of Mr. Custis's will." These were owned by Mrs. Lee.[155]

George Washington Parke Custis, his father-in-law, died Saturday, October 10, 1857. In his will he provided that all his slaves should be set free after the expiration of five years. Robert E. Lee was named as executor. The time came in 1863, "when the flames of war were fiercely raging," while General Lee was at Fredericksburg. Notwithstanding the exacting duties incident to the position of army commander, the care of suffering soldiers, and his anxiety about their future, immediate and distant, he proceeded according to the law of the land to carry out the provisions of the will. He summoned them together, as far as possible, within his lines and delivered to them their free papers, as well as passes through the Confederate lines to go whither they would.[156]

He wrote thus of them to Mrs. Lee:

They are entitled to their freedom, and I wish to give it to them. Those that have been carried away, I hope are free and happy; I cannot get their papers to them, and they do not require them. I will give them if they ever call for them.[157]

Many of them had been carried off by the Northern men.

Lee is recorded as saying that, if he owned all the Negroes of the South, he would gladly yield them up for the preservation of the Union.[158] Lee was "in favor of freeing all the slaves in the South, giving to each owner a bond to be the first paid by the Confederacy when its independence should be secured."[159]

Letter to Daughter Agnes

In a letter to his daughter Agnes, Friday, February 6, 1863, from "Camp Fredericksburg," Virginia, he told of the hard winter, sufferings, etc., and then closed: "I must stop and go to work. See how kind God is; we have plenty to do in good weather and bad."[160]

Fast Day

In closing his general order for the observance of the fast day appointed by President Davis in the spring of 1863, Lee made the following earnest appeal:

Soldiers! No portion of our people have greater cause to be thankful to Almighty God than yourselves. He has preserved your lives amidst countless dangers. He has been with you in all your trials. He has given you fortitude under hardships and courage in the shock of battle. He has cheered you by the example and by the deeds of your martyred comrades. He has enabled you to defend your country successfully against the assaults of a powerful oppressor. Devoutly thankful for signal mercies, let us bow before the Lord of hosts and join our hearts with millions in our land in prayer that He will continue His merciful protection over our cause; that He will scatter our enemies and set at naught their evil designs, and that He will graciously restore to our country the blessings of peace and security.[161]

Lee and Jackson at Church

Rev. Dr. George W. Leyburn, Presbyterian missionary, in telling of some religious meetings in the army, spoke of a great meeting in the "war-battered town of Fredericksburg," on a Sabbath morning in the spring of 1863. It was at General "Stonewall" Jackson's headquarters. At least a thousand soldiers were present. "It was one of the most brilliant and noble assemblies of military men ever brought together. Beside Generals Lee and Jackson, I remember that Early and Kershaw were there, and a host of officers of various rank."[162]

"Stonewall" Jackson Wounded

"Stonewall" Jackson was wounded at the

battle of Chancellorsville, "the greatest of General Lee's battles." Hearing that he was worse, General Lee said, "Tell him that I am praying for him as I believe I have never prayed for myself."[163]

Sunday, May 10, 1863, General Lee was present at the service conducted by the Rev. B. T. Lacy, of General Jackson's staff. He inquired particularly about General Jackson's condition. Upon being told that he would probably not live through the day, General Lee exclaimed:

Oh, sir, he must not die. Surely God will not visit us with such a calamity. If I have ever prayed in my life, I have pleaded with the Lord that Jackson might be spared to us.[164]

Battle of Chancellorsville

In his dispatch to President Davis, after Chancellorsville, he said, "We have again to thank Almighty God for a great victory."[165]

Only Giver of Victory

Thursday, May 7, 1863, in a congratulatory address to the army after the battle of Chancellorsville, he said:

While this glorious victory entitles you to the praises and gratitude of the nation, we are especially called upon to return our grateful thanks to the only Giver of victory for the signal deliverance He wrought.

It is therefore earnestly recommended that the troops unite on Sunday next in ascribing unto the Lord of Hosts the glory due unto His name.[166]

Death of "Stonewall" Jackson

Monday, May 11, 1863, he issued an order announcing "the death of Lieutenant General T. J. Jackson," saying:

The daring skill and energy of this great and good soldier, by the decrees of an all-wise Providence, are now lost to us. But while we mourn his death, we feel that his spirit still lives and will inspire the whole army with his indomitable courage and unshaken confidence in God as our hope and strength.[167]

"God's Will Be Done"

General Lee wrote of this event to Mrs. Lee in Richmond, from Camp Fredericksburg, Monday, May 11, 1863:

In addition to the death of officers and friends consequent upon the late battle, you will see we have to mourn the loss of the great and good Jackson. Any victory will be dear at such a price. His remains go to Richmond to-day. I know not how to replace him. God's will be done! I trust He will raise up someone in his place.[168]

CHAPTER X

GOD HIS HELPER

Trust in God Alone

The Rev. Dr. T. V. Moore, so long pastor of the First Presbyterian Church of Richmond, Virginia, related the following in a memorial discourse in the First Presbyterian Church, Nashville, Tennessee, of which he was then the pastor, Sunday, October 23, 1870, eleven days after General Lee's death:

"About the middle of the war, when the horizon looked very dark, I spent an evening with him, at the house of a friend, and he was evidently, in spite of his habitual self-command, deeply depressed. Happening to be alone with him, as we parted for the night, I endeavored to cheer him with the fact that so many Christian people were praying for him. I shall never forget the emphasis with which he grasped my hand as, with voice and eye that betrayed deep emotion, he assured me that it (knowledge of prayer) was not only his comfort, but his only comfort, and declared the simple and absolute trust that he had in God and God alone, as his helper in that terrible struggle."[169]

GOD HIS HELPER

Attends Prayers

The Rev. Kensey Johns Stewart, a chaplain in the Confederate Army, who married a first cousin of General Lee, related this incident:

"At Leesburg the other day I was seated in the drawing room of a house there, with the family, officers staying there and others, collected for prayers. Generals Lee and Jackson were in an upper room, in close consultation, with the door locked. I sent a message to them to come down to prayers. General Chilton, who was Lee's adjutant-general, took the message to them. I had before me the family Bible, which had been brought in and placed on a little stand before me, and I went on with the service. The two generals came down and took seats a little behind me. And I heard afterward from a lady who was present and sat near them, that, as they rose from their knees, the traces of tears were on the faces of both Lee and Jackson. Many wondered at my having the boldness to interrupt them in their consultation. Not an officer present would have dared to do it."[170]

Praying on the Eve of Battle

"While the Army of Northern Virginia confronted General Meade at Mine Run, near the end of November, 1863, and a battle was momentarily expected, General Lee, with a number of general and staff officers, was riding down his line of battle, when, just in the rear of General A. P. Hill's position, the cavalcade suddenly came upon a party of soldiers engaged in one of those prayer meetings which they so often held on the eve of battle. An attack from the enemy seemed imminent—already the sharpshooting along the skirmish-line had begun—the artillery was belching forth its hoarse thunder, and the mind and heart of the great chieftain were full of the expected combat. Yet, as he saw those ragged veterans bowed in prayer, he instantly dismounted, uncovered his head and devoutly joined in the simple worship. The rest of the party at once followed his example, and those humble privates found themselves leading the devotions of their loved and honored chieftain."[171]

Will Not Disturb Prayer Meeting

He forbade his staff to disturb an impromptu prayer meeting which stopped their way when hurrying to the fierce battle in the Wilderness.[172]

Evolution

One night some soldiers were overheard discussing the tenets of atheism around their camp fire, when a rough, honest fellow cut short the discussion by saying, "Well, boys, the rest of us may have developed from monkeys; but I tell you none less than a God could have made such a man as 'Marse Robert!'"[173]

Merciful Father

On Sunday, May 31, 1863, when he was ready for active operations after the winter's rest, Lee wrote to Mrs. Lee: "I pray that our merciful Father in heaven may protect and direct us. In that case I fear no odds and no numbers."[174]

God's Beautiful World

Monday, June 8, 1863, the day after the grand review of the cavalry corps, about eight thousand well-mounted men, he writes:

The country here looks very green and pretty, notwithstanding the ravages of war. What a beautiful world God, in His loving-kindness to His creatures, has given us! What a shame that men endowed with reason and knowledge of right should mar His gifts![175]

Son Fitzhugh Wounded

His son, Major-General William H. F. (Fitzhugh) Lee, was wounded on Tuesday, June 9, 1863, in the famous battle of Brandy Station, and was sent to "Hickory Hill," a place about twenty miles from Richmond, to recover. General Lee wrote to Fitzhugh's wife on Thursday, June 11:

I know that you will unite with me in thanks to Almighty God, who has so often sheltered him in the hour of danger, for his recent deliverance, and lift up your whole heart in praise to Him for sparing a life so dear to us, while enabling him to do his duty in the station in which He had placed him. Ask him to join us in supplication that He may always cover him with the shadow of His almighty arm and teach him that his only refuge is in Him, the greatness of whose mercy reacheth unto the heavens, and His truth unto the clouds.[176]

No Bitterness

General Lee uttered no word of personal bitterness toward the people of the North. He referred to them as "those people" or as "our friends across the river." During the war "he did not for a single moment forget that he led the army of a people who professed to be governed by the principles of Christian civilization, and that no outrages on the part of others could justify him in departing from these high principles."[177]

A Humane Commander

On Saturday, June 27, 1863, the day succeeding his arrival at Chambersburg, Pennsyl-

GOD HIS HELPER

vania, General Lee issued the following order to his army:

The Commanding General has observed with marked satisfaction the conduct of the troops on the march and confidently anticipates results commensurate with the high spirit they have manifested. No troops could have displayed greater fortitude or better performed the arduous marches of the past ten days. Their conduct in other respects has, with few exceptions, been in keeping with their character as soldiers and entitles them to approbation and praise.

There have, however, been instances of forgetfulness on the part of some that they have in keeping the yet unsullied reputation of the army, and that the duties exacted of us by civilization and Christianity are not less obligatory in the country of the enemy than in our own. The Commanding General considers that no greater disgrace could befall the army, and through it our whole people, than the perpetration of the barbarous outrages upon the innocent and defenseless and the wanton destruction of private property that have marked the course of the enemy in our own country. Such proceedings not only disgrace the perpetrators and all connected with them, but are subversive of the discipline and efficiency of the army, and destructive of the ends of our present movements. It must be remembered that we make war only upon armed men, and that we cannot take vengeance for the wrongs our people have suffered without lowering ourselves in the eyes of all whose abhorrence has been excited by the atrocities of our enemy, and offending against Him to whom vengeance belongeth, without whose favor and support our efforts must all prove in vain.

The Commanding General, therefore, earnestly exhorts the troops to abstain, with most scrupulous care, from unnecessary or wanton injury to private property; and he enjoins upon all officers to arrest and bring to summary punishment all who shall in any way offend against the orders on this subject.[178]

Battle of Gettysburg

Following the battle of Gettysburg, in an order issued to the army from his headquarters at Hagerstown, Maryland, Saturday, July 11, 1863, Lee said:

Let each heart grow strong in the remembrance of our glorious part and in the thought of the inestimable blessings for which we contend; and invoking the assistance of that Heavenly Power which has so signally blessed our former efforts, let us go forth in confidence to secure the peace and safety of our country.[179]

CHAPTER XI

THE HEART OF LEE

A Wounded Northern Soldier

Long after the war a Northern Grand Army man told of meeting Lee in the field at Gettysburg under circumstances which revealed to him the true heart of the Southern commander:

"I had been a most bitter anti-South man, and fought and cursed the Confederates desperately. I could see nothing good in any of them. The last day of the fight I was badly wounded. A ball shattered my left leg. I lay on the ground not far from Cemetery Ridge, and as General Lee ordered his retreat, he and his officers rode near me.

"As they came along I recognized him, and, though faint from exposure and loss of blood, I raised my hands, and looked Lee in the face, and shouted as loud as I could—'Hurrah for the Union!'

"The General heard me, looked, stopped his horse, dismounted, and came toward me. I confess I at first thought he meant to kill me. But, as he came up, he looked down at me with such a sad expression upon his face that

114   ROBERT E. LEE THE CHRISTIAN

all fear left me, and I wondered what he was about. He extended his hand to me, grasping mine firmly, and looking right into my eyes, said:

" 'My son, I hope you will soon be well.'

"If I live a thousand years, I shall never forget the expression on General Lee's face. There he was, defeated, retiring from a field that had cost him and his cause almost their last hope, and yet he stopped to say words like these to a wounded soldier of the opposition who had taunted him as he passed by! As soon as the General had left me, I cried myself to sleep there on the bloody ground."[130]

Submit to God's Will

On Sunday, July 12, 1863, from near Hagerstown, he wrote to his wife:

The consequences of war are horrid enough at best, surrounded by all the ameliorations of civilization and Christianity. . . . You will, however, learn before this reaches you that our success at Gettysburg was not so great as reported—in fact, that we failed to drive the enemy from his position and that our army withdrew to the Potomac. Had the river not unexpectedly risen, all would have been well with us; but God, in His all-wise providence, willed otherwise, and our communications have been interrupted and almost cut off. The waters have subsided to about four feet, and, if they continue, by to-morrow, I hope, our communications will be open.

I trust that a merciful God, our only hope and refuge, will not desert us in this hour of need, and will deliver us by His almighty hand, that the whole world may recognize His power and all hearts be lifted up in adoration and praise of His unbounded loving-kindness. We must, however, submit to His almighty will, whatever that may be. May God guide and protect us all is my constant prayer.[181]

Implores Forgiveness of God

On Wednesday, July 15, 1863, he wrote from Bunker Hill, Virginia, to his wife, closing:

I hope we will yet be able to damage our adversaries when they meet us. That it should be so we must implore the forgiveness of God for our sins, and the continuance of His blessings. There is nothing but His almighty power that can sustain us. God bless you all.[182]

Paying Taxes

Shortly after the battle of Gettysburg, Lee wrote the following:

I have been much exercised as to how I can pay my taxes. I have looked out for assessors and gatherers in vain. I have sent to find collectors in the counties where I have been, without success.

I wish to pay the amount as a matter of right and conscience, and for the benefit of the state, but cannot accomplish it. In addition, I own three horses, a watch, my apparel, and camp equipage. See if you can find some one that can enlighten me as to what I am to pay.[183]

Son Fitzhugh Captured

While slowly recovering from his wound, about two weeks after his arrival at "Hickory Hill," his son Fitzhugh was captured by a raiding party of the enemy and carried, before the astonished wife and relatives, to prison at Fortress Monroe. General Lee wrote the following letter to the son's wife soon after, Sunday, July 26, 1863, from Camp Culpeper, Virginia:

I can appreciate your distress at F——'s situation. I deeply sympathize with it, and in the lone hours of the night, I groan in sorrow at his captivity and separation from you. But we must all bear it, exercise all our patience, and do nothing to aggravate the evil. This, besides injuring ourselves, would rejoice our enemies and be sinful in the eyes of God. In His own good time He will relieve us and make all things work together for our good, if we give Him our love, and place in Him our trust. . . . You may think of F——, and love him as much as you please, but do not grieve over him or grow sad. That will not be right, you precious child!... Indeed, the loss of our gallant officers and men throughout the army causes me to weep tears of blood and to wish that I never could hear the sound of a gun again. My only consolation is that they are happier, and we that are left are to be pitied....

You must think of me, and pray for me always, and know that I am always thinking of you.... May God in His great mercy guard and protect you and your dear husband![184]

"Not Repine at Will of God"

From Williamsport, Virginia, to Fitzhugh's mother, he thus wrote of their son's capture:

I have heard with great grief that Fitzhugh has been captured by the enemy. Had not expected that he would be taken from his bed and carried off, but we must bear this additional affliction with fortitude and resignation, and not repine at the will of God. It will eventuate in some good that we know not of now. We must bear our labors and hardships manfully. Our noble men are cheerful and confident. I constantly remember you in my thoughts and prayers.[185]

Day of Fasting

On Thursday, August 13, 1863, Lee issued the following order:

The President of the Confederate States has, in the name of the people, appointed August 21 as a

1863] [Age 56

day of fasting, humiliation, and prayer. A strict observance of the day is enjoined upon the officers and soldiers of this army. All military duties, except such as are absolutely necessary, will be suspended. The commanding officers of brigades and regiments are requested to cause divine services suitable to the occasion, to be performed in their respective commands. Soldiers! We have sinned against Almighty God. We have forgotten His signal mercies and have cultivated a revengeful, haughty, and boastful spirit. We have not remembered that the defenders of a just cause should be pure in His eyes; that "our times are in His hands," and we have relied too much on our own arms for the achievement of our independence.

God is our only refuge and our strength. Let us humble ourselves before Him. Let us confess our many sins and beseech Him to give us a higher courage, a purer patriotism and more determined will; that He will convert the hearts of our enemies; that He will hasten the time when war, with its sorrows and sufferings, shall cease, and that He will give us a name and place among the nations of the earth.[186]

Effect of the Order

Chaplain J. William Jones says:

"I can never forget the effect produced by the reading of this order at the solemn services of that memorable fast-day. A revival was already in progress in many of the commands

—the day was almost universally observed—
the attendance upon preaching and other services was very large. The solemn attention and
starting tear attested the deep interest felt,
and the work of grace among the troops widened
and deepened and went gloriously on until
over fifteen thousand of the soldiers of Lee's
army professed repentance toward God and
faith in Jesus Christ as a personal Saviour.
How far these results were due to this fast-day,
or to the quiet influence and fervent prayers of
the commanding general, eternity alone shall
reveal."[187]

Great Revival in Army

There was at this time a great revival of
religion in the army. General Lee became
much interested in it, and did what he could
to promote in his camps all sacred exercises.

"A devout Christian himself, he thought of
each man in his army as a soul to be saved, and
in every way he could, encouraged the mission
and revival work which went on all through
the war with ever-increasing activity. Even
in the midst of urgent duty he would stop
and take part in a camp prayer meeting
and listen to the exhortations of some ragged
veteran, as a young convert might listen to an
apostle."[188]

1863] [Age 56

"Not a chaplain in his army excelled him in personal piety or in devoutness."

Promoted Revivals

It was due in large measure to Lee's influence as a Christian commander that great revivals often occurred in the army. Chaplain J. William Jones says: "It is believed that no army in the world's history ever had in it so much of genuine, devout piety, so much of active work for Christ, as the Army of Northern Virginia, under the command of our noble Christian leader."

So concerned was Lee for the spiritual welfare of his soldiers that one of his biographers says, "One almost feels as if he cared more for winning souls than battles, and for supplying his army with Bibles than with bullets and powder."[189]

He was ardent in worship both private and public. Such a curious religious democracy as prevailed in his army has probably not been seen in the world since the days of Cromwell.[190]

"Time and again during the war a wave of spiritual awakening swept over the army whose head was the most pious and devout Christian that any army ever followed." There were thousands of genuine conversions.

THE HEART OF LEE

Hope in God

Tuesday, September 18, 1863, from camp near Orange Court House, Virginia, he wrote to his wife:

The enemy state that they have heard of a great reduction in our forces here, and are now going to drive us back to Richmond. I trust they will not succeed; but our hope and refuge is in our merciful Father in heaven.[191]

Sympathy for Soldiers

On Friday, October 9, 1863, the Army of Northern Virginia was put in motion, pushing back the Northern Army. From "Camp Rappahannock," Virginia, Sunday, October 25, 1863, Lee wrote to his wife:

I could have thrown him [General Meade] farther back, but saw no chance of bringing him to battle, and it would only have served to fatigue our troops by advancing farther. I should certainly have endeavored to throw them north of the Potomac; but thousands were barefooted, thousands with fragments of shoes, and all without overcoats, blankets, or warm clothing. I could not bear to expose them to certain suffering and an uncertain issue.[192]

Prayer for Nephews

Sunday, November 1, 1863, he wrote from "Camp Rappahannock," to his wife, in which he told of a visit from three nephews, who were "on a little expedition." He said, "As soon as I was left alone, I committed them in a fervent prayer to the care of and guidance of our Heavenly Father."[193]

"All Things for Our Good"

In a letter to his wife from "Camp Rapidan," Virginia, Friday, December 4, 1863, he said, "I believe a kind God has ordered all things for our good."[194]

Declines Mansion in Richmond

In November, 1863, the City Council of Richmond passed a resolution to purchase for Lee an elegant mansion, as a small token of the high esteem in which he was held by the city which he had so long defended. "Arlington" was in the hands of the United States government, the "White House" on York River [the house of Washington's early wedded life] had been ruthlessly burned by Federal soldiers, his splendid estate had nearly all passed from his control, and his salary in Confederate scrip was utterly inadequate to support in proper style his invalid wife and accomplished daughters. These facts were known to the city authorities, and they but reflected the popular wish in the action which they took.

But, when General Lee heard of it, he wrote as follows to the president of the Council:

I assure you, sir, that no want of appreciation of the honor conferred upon me by this resolution, or insensibility to the kind feelings which prompted it, induces me to ask, as I most respectfully do, that no further proceedings be taken with reference to the subject. The house is not necessary to the use of my family, and my own duties will prevent my residence in Richmond.

I should, therefore, be compelled to decline the generous offer, and I trust that whatever means the City Council may have to spare for this purpose may be devoted to the relief of the families of our soldiers in the field, who are more in want of assistance, and more deserving of it, than myself.[195]

Death of Daughter-in-Law

About this time occurred the death of his daughter-in-law, whose husband, Major-General W. H. F. Lee, was kept a prisoner at Fortress Monroe for nine long, weary months. General Benjamin F. Butler, in charge, refused to allow the husband to visit his dying wife, although his brother, Custis Lee, of equal rank, had volunteered in writing to take his place for forty-eight hours as a hostage, until the brother should return to his captivity. The wife died calling for her captive husband.

124 ROBERT E. LEE THE CHRISTIAN

In a letter to his wife, Sunday, December 27, 1863, General Lee said:

Custis's [his son] dispatch which I received last night demolished all the hopes, in which I had been indulging during the day, of dear Charlotte's recovery. It has pleased God to take from us one exceedingly dear to us, and we must be resigned to His holy will. She, I trust, will enjoy peace and happiness forever, while we must patiently struggle on under all the ills that may be in store for us. What a glorious thought it is that she has joined her little cherubs [two infants] and our angel Annie [his second daughter] in heaven! Thus link by link is the strong chain broken that binds us to earth, and our passage soothed to another world.

Oh, that we may be at last united in that heaven of rest, where trouble and sorrow never enter, to join in an everlasting chorus of praise and glory to our Lord and Saviour! I grieve for our lost darling as a father only can grieve for a daughter, and my sorrow is heightened by the thought of the anguish her death will cause our dear son and the poignancy it will give the bars of his prison. May God in His mercy enable him to bear the blow He has so suddenly dealt, and sanctify it to his everlasting happiness![196]

His love for her was like that for his own children, and when her husband was captured and thrown, wounded, into prison, his great tenderness for her was shown on all occasions.

Her death, though expected, was a great blow to him.

Note that there was no word of bitterness against General Butler, the most hated Northern general in all the South.

CHAPTER XII

SABBATH OBSERVANCE

INTERVIEW ON SABBATH OBSERVANCE

CHAPLAIN J. WILLIAM JONES relates the following:

"I can never forget my interview and conversation with General Lee on religious matters. It was on Saturday, February 6, 1864, while our army was resting along the Rapidan, that the Rev. B. T. Lacey, 'Stonewall' Jackson's chaplain, and myself went, as a committee of our Chaplains' Association, to consult him in reference to the better observance of the Sabbath in the army, and especially to urge that something be done to prevent irreligious officers from converting Sunday into a grand gala day for inspections, reviews, etc. It was a delicate mission. We did not wish to appear either as informers or officious intermeddlers, and yet we were anxious to do something to further the wishes of those who sent us and to put a stop to what was then a growing evil and, in some commands, a serious obstacle to the efficient work of the chaplain.

"The cordial greeting which he gave us, the

marked courtesy and respect with which he listened to what we had to say and expressed his warm sympathy with the object of our mission, soon put us at our ease. But as we presently began to answer his questions concerning the spiritual interests of the army, and to tell of that great revival which was then extending through the camps and bringing thousands of our noble men to Christ, we saw his eye brighten and his whole countenance glow with pleasure; and as, in his simple, feeling words, he expressed his delight, we forgot the great warrior and only remembered that we were communing with an humble, earnest Christian.

"As we were about to leave his tent, Mr. Lacey said:

"'I think it right that I should say to you, General, that the chaplains of this army have a deep interest in your welfare and that some of the most fervent prayers we offer are in your behalf.' The old hero's face flushed, tears started in his eyes, and he replied, with choked utterance and deep emotion:

"Please thank them for that, sir—I warmly appreciate it. And I can only say that I am nothing but a poor sinner, trusting in Christ alone for salvation, and need all of the prayers they can offer for me."[197]

1864] [Age 57

ROBERT E. LEE THE CHRISTIAN

Another Order for Sabbath Observance

The day after the interview he issued the following:

Headquarters, Army of Northern Virginia, February 7 (Sunday), 1864.
General Order No. 15.

I. The attention of the army already has been called to the obligation of a proper observance of the Sabbath; but the sense of its importance, not only as a moral and religious duty, but as contributing to the personal health and well-being of the troops, induces the Commanding General to repeat the orders on that subject. He has learned with great pleasure that in many brigades convenient houses of worship have been erected, and earnestly desires that every facility consistent with the requirements of discipline shall be afforded men to assemble themselves together for the purpose of devotion.

II. To this end he directs that none but duties strictly necessary shall be required to be performed on Sunday, and that labor, both of men and animals, which it is practicable to anticipate or postpone, or the immediate performance of which is not essential to safety, health, or comfort of the army, shall be suspended on that day.

III. Commanding officers will require the usual inspection on Sunday to be held at such time as not to interfere with the attendance of men on divine service at the customary hour in the morning.

SABBATH OBSERVANCE

IV. They will also give their attention to the maintenance of order and quiet around the place of worship and prohibit anything that may tend to disturb or interrupt religious exercises.

R. E. LEE, *General*.[198]

DAY OF FASTING

Wednesday, March 30, 1864, Lee issued orders to the army directing the observance of Friday, April 8, "as a day of fasting, humiliation, and prayer," in accordance with a proclamation by President Davis. He said:

The Commanding General invites the army to join in the observance of the day. He directs due preparation to be made in all departments to anticipate the wants of the several commands so that it may be strictly observed. All military duties, except such as are absolutely necessary, will be suspended. The chaplains are desired to hold services in their regiments and brigades. The officers and men are requested to attend.

Soldiers! Let us humble ourselves before the Lord, our God, asking through Christ, the forgiveness of our sins, beseeching the aid of the God of our forefathers in the defense of our homes and our liberties, thanking Him for His past blessings, and imploring their continuance upon our cause and our people.[199]

General Lee observed the day reverently.

God's Almighty Arm

On Sunday, April 24, 1864, General Lee wrote to his cousin, Miss Margaret Stuart, of whom he was very fond, from Camp Orange County, Virginia:

I dislike to send letters within reach of the enemy, as they might serve, if captured, to bring distress on others; but you must sometimes cast your thoughts on the Army of Northern Virginia, and never forget it in your pious prayers. It is preparing for a great struggle, but I pray and trust that the great God, mighty to deliver, will spread over it His Almighty arm and drive its enemies before it.[200]

CHAPTER XIII

UNSELFISH NOBLENESS

Declined Special Exchange for His Son

The Rev. Dr. T. V. Moore, at that time pastor of the First Presbyterian Church in Nashville, Tennessee, related the following in his memorial sermon on Sunday afternoon, October 23, 1870:

"After the cartel for the exchange of prisoners during the war was suspended, one of his own sons [Fitzhugh] was taken prisoner. A Federal officer of the same rank in Libby Prison sent for me, and wished me to write to General Lee, begging him to obtain the consent of the Confederate authorities to his release, provided he could, as he felt sure would be the case, induce the United States authorities to send General Lee's son through the lines to effect this special exchange.

"In a few days a reply was received in which, with the lofty spirit of a Roman Brutus, he respectfully but firmly declined *to ask any favor for his own son that could not be asked for the humblest soldier in the army.* The officer, while disappointed, was yet so struck with the unselfish nobleness of the reply, that he begged the letter from me as a memento of General Lee, adding, with deep emphasis, 'Sir, I regard him as the greatest man now living.'"

It will add greatly to the force of the above incident to recall the fact that the son [General W. H. F. Lee] was at home, severely wounded, at the time he was captured; that his accomplished wife was lying at the point of death and actually died before his release (the Federal authorities refusing to allow General Custis Lee to take the place of his brother, as he nobly offered to do) and that he was closely confined in a casemate at Fortress Monroe and threatened with death by hanging in retaliation for alleged cruelty on the part of the Confederate authorities toward certain Federal prisoners.

"Only those who know how devoted to his children General Lee was can appreciate the noble self-denial which he exercised when, under these circumstances, the tenderest feelings of the loving father were sacrificed to his sense of duty to his country."[201]

His Great Grief

General Lee was deeply attached to his son's wife, and wrote her many touchingly beautiful letters, full of the consolations and hopes of

UNSELFISH NOBLENESS

the gospel. When she died, as has been noted, while her husband (General W. H. F. Lee) was in a Northern prison, at Fortress Monroe, the General's son was plunged into deepest grief. On his return from prison, General Lee wrote him the following Sunday, April 23, 1864, on the eve of the great campaign of 1864:

I received last night, my dear son, your letter of the 22nd. It has given me great comfort. God knows how I loved your dear, dear wife, how sweet her memory is to me, and how I mourn her loss. My grief could not be greater if you had been taken from me. You were both equally dear to me. My heart is too full to speak on this subject, nor can I write. But my grief is for ourselves, not for her. She is brighter and happier than ever —safe from all evil and awaiting us in her heavenly abode. May God in His mercy enable us to join her in eternal praise to our Lord and Saviour. Let us humbly bow ourselves before Him, and offer perpetual prayer for pardon and forgiveness.

But we cannot indulge in grief, however mournfully pleasing. Our country demands all our strength, all our energies. To resist the powerful combination now forming against us will require every man at his place. If victorious, we have everything to hope for in the future. If defeated, nothing will be left for us to live for. I have not heard what action has been taken by the department in reference to my recommendations concerning the organization of the cavalry. But we have no time to wait, and you had better join your brigade. This week will, in all probability, bring us active work, and we must strike fast and strong. My whole trust is in God, and I am ready for whatever He may ordain. May He guide, guard, and strengthen us, is my constant prayer."[202]

Self-Denial

Chaplain J. William Jones says:

"General Lee rarely slept in a house—never outside of his lines—during the war, and when on the march some convenient fence-corner would be his most frequent place of bivouac. The writer has not infrequently seen some colonel, or major-quartermaster, entertained in princely style at some hospitable mansion, while near by the commander-in-chief would bivouac in the open air.

"He never allowed his mess to draw from the commissary more than they were entitled to, and not infrequently he would sit down to a dinner meager in quality and scant in quantity."[203]

Interest in Welfare of Men

Lee always manifested the liveliest interest in the welfare of his men, and was deeply touched by their hardships and privations. Being invited upon one occasion to dine at a house where an elegant dinner was served, it is related that he declined all of the rich viands offered him, dined on bread and beef, and quietly said in explanation to the lady of the house, "I cannot consent to be feasting while my poor soldiers are nearly starving."

Sweet potatoes and buttermilk made him a satisfactory meal, while his dinner often consisted of cabbage boiled with a little salt. Once General Lee offered his luncheon to a major-general. It was found to consist of two cold, roasted sweet potatoes, of which Lee said that he was very fond.[204]

In the same spirit he wrote to some young officers who were getting up a grand military ball:

I do not think this a fit time for feasting or unseemly merrymaking. I am always gratified to see your names figure among the gallant defenders of the country. I confess that I have no desire just now to see them conspicuous among the promoters of a "Grand Military Ball," or anything of that character.[205]

Interest in Work of Chaplains

General Lee always took the deepest interest in the work of his chaplains and the spiritual welfare of his men. He was a frequent visitor at the chaplains' meetings, and a deeply interested observer of their proceedings; and the faithful chaplain who stuck to his post and did his duty could be always assured of a warm friend at headquarters.[206]

Always Attended Preaching

He never failed to attend preaching when his duties did not absolutely preclude his doing so. Nor was he a mere listless attendant. The simple truths of the gospel had no more attentive listener than General Lee; and his eyes would kindle and his face glow under the more tender doctrines of grace. He used frequently to attend preaching at Jackson's headquarters; and it was a scene which a master-hand might have delighted to paint—those two great warriors, surrounded by hundreds of officers and men, bowed in humble worship before the God and Saviour in whom they trusted.[207]

Rides to Richmond

When encamped near Richmond, General Lee would ride into the city on Traveller before breakfast for early Sunday morning service, which lasted not over a half hour, then ride back to camp for breakfast.[208]

Death of General Stuart

In his order announcing the death of Gen-

UNSELFISH NOBLENESS

eral J. E. B. Stuart, his great cavalry leader, which occurred on Thursday, May 12, 1864, Lee said:

To his military capacity of a high order and to the noble virtues of the soldier he added the brighter graces of a pure life, guided and sustained by the Christian's faith and hope. The mysterious hand of an all-wise God has removed him from the scene of his usefulness and fame.[209]

Grieves Over Loss of Men

In a letter to his wife, from Spotsylvania Court House, Virginia, Monday, May 16, 1864, he said:

As I write I am expecting the sound of the guns every moment. I grieve over the loss of our gallant officers and men and miss their aid and sympathy. A more zealous, ardent, brave, and devoted soldier than Stuart the Confederacy cannot have. Praise be to God for having sustained us so far. I have thought of you very often in these eventful days. God bless and preserve you.[210]

Divine Service Under the Trees

Sunday, July 10, 1864, writing from Camp Petersburg, Virginia, to his daughter Mildred, he said:

Mr. Platt, pastor of the principal Episcopal church, had services at my headquarters to-day.

138 ROBERT E. LEE THE CHRISTIAN

The services were under the trees, and the discourse on the subject of salvation.[211]

Friday, June 24, 1864, writing from Camp Petersburg, to his wife, he said:

Mr. Platt had services again to-day under the trees near my camp. We had quite a large congregation of citizens, ladies and gentlemen, and our usual number of soldiers. During the services I constantly heard the shells crashing among the houses of Petersburg.[212]

Anniversary of Wedding

Thursday, June 30, 1864, the anniversary of his wedding day, he wrote to his wife:

I was glad to receive your letter yesterday, and to hear that you were better. I trust that you will continue to improve and soon be as well as usual. God grant that you may be entirely restored in His own good time. Do you recollect what a happy day thirty-three years ago this was? How many hopes and pleasures it gave birth to! God has been very merciful and kind to us, and how thankless and sinful I have been! I pray that He may continue His mercies and blessings to us and give us a little peace and rest together in this world, and finally gather us and all He has given us around His throne in the world to come.[213]

Destruction of Churches

Sunday, August 14, 1864, he wrote from Camp Petersburg to his wife at Richmond:

UNSELFISH NOBLENESS 139

I have been kept from church to-day by the enemy's crossing to the north side of the James River and the necessity of moving troops to meet him. . . . I received to-day a kind letter from the Rev. Mr. Cole, of Culpeper Court House. He is a most excellent man in all the relations of life. He says there is not a church standing in all that country, within the lines formerly occupied by the enemy. All are razed to the ground, and the materials used often for the vilest purposes. Two of the churches at the Court House barely escaped destruction. The pews were all taken out to make seats for the theater. The fact was reported to the commanding officer by their own men of the Christian Commission, but he took no steps to rebuke or arrest it. We must suffer patiently to the end, when all things will be made right.[214]

CHAPTER XIV

A KNEELING CHRISTIAN

Little Girl in Church With General

WHILE at Petersburg, in the winter of 1864, Lee attended preaching one day at a crowded chapel and noticed a little girl, dressed in faded garments, standing just inside the door and timidly looking around for a seat. "Come with me, my little lady," said the great soldier, "and you shall sit by me." And taking the little girl by the hand he secured her a comfortable seat at his side.[215]

Kneels in the Dust

It is related that, as his army was crossing the James, in June, 1864, and hurrying on to meet Grant at Petersburg, General Lee, with a thousand cares and duties on his shoulders, turned aside from the road, and kneeling in the dust beside a minister, devoutly joined in earnest prayer that God would give him wisdom and grace in the new stage of the campaign upon which he was then entering.[216]

"Let us go some bright Sabbath morning," writes Chaplain J. William Jones, "to that

A KNEELING CHRISTIAN

cluster of tents in the grove across the Massaponax, not far from Hamiltons Crossing. Seated on the rude logs, or on the ground, may be seen fifteen hundred or two thousand men, with upturned faces, eagerly drinking in the truths of the gospel. That reverent worshiper who kneels in the dust during prayer, or listens with sharpened attention and moist eyes as the preacher delivers his message, is our loved Commander-in-Chief, General R. E. Lee."

Tracts and Prayer Books

Chaplain J. William Jones relates the following:

"Not long before the evacuation of Petersburg, Virginia, I was one day on the lines not far above Hatchers Run busily engaged in distributing tracts and religious newspapers, which the soldiers were eagerly crowding around to get, when I saw a large cavalcade approaching. As they drew near, I recognized Generals Lee, A. P. Hill, Gordon, Heth, and several other generals, who, accompanied by a large staff, were inspecting the lines. I stepped aside to let the cavalcade pass, but the keen eye of Gordon recognized and his cordial grasp detained me while he eagerly inquired about my work. General Lee reined in his noble steed

(Traveller) and joined in the conversation, the rest all gathered around, and the humble tract distributor found himself the center of a group whose names and deeds shine on the brightest pages of the history they contributed so much to make.

"My old colonel, now Lieutenant-General A. P. Hill, and one of the most accomplished soldiers, as well as one of the most high-toned gentlemen whom the war produced, pleasantly asked of me, as he gave me a hearty greeting, 'John' (as he always familiarly called me), 'don't you think the boys would prefer "hardtack" to tracts just now?'

"'I have no doubt that many of them would,' I replied; but they crowd around and take the tracts as eagerly as they surround the commissary, when he has anything to "issue," and, besides other advantages, the tracts certainly help them to bear the lack of "hardtack."'

"'I have no doubt of it,' he said, 'and I am glad you are able to supply the tracts more abundantly than we can the rations.'

"General Lee asked me if I ever had calls for prayer-books among the soldiers. I told him that I frequently had, and he replied:

Well, you would greatly oblige me if you would call at my quarters and get and distribute a few

A KNEELING CHRISTIAN

which I have. I bought a new one when in Richmond the other day, and upon my saying that I would give my old one, which I had carried through the Mexican War and had kept ever since, to some soldiers, the bookseller offered to give me a dozen new prayer-books for the old one. I, of course, accepted so good an offer; and now I have a dozen to give away instead of one.

"I called at the appointed hour; the General had been called away from his quarters on some important matter, but he had (even amid his pressing cares and responsibilities) left the prayer-books with a member of his staff, with directions concerning them. In each one he had written, in his own well-known handwriting, 'Presented to ──── by R. E. Lee.' "[217]

THANKFUL FOR PRAYERS

The Rev. Dr. T. V. Moore tells how General Lee never failed to acknowledge a kindness:

"During the summer of 1864 . . . I had occasion to render him a slight service, so slight that, knowing at the time that he was sick and overburdened with responsibilities of his arduous and continually menaced position, I never expected it to be acknowledged at all; but, to my surprise, I received a letter thanking me for this trivial service, and adding:

I thank you especially that I have a place in your

prayers. No human power can avail us without the blessing of God, and I rejoice to know that, in this crisis of our affairs, good men everywhere are supplicating Him for His favor and protection.[218]

Jewish Furloughs Requested Again

Tuesday, September 20, 1864, Lee replied to another request from Rabbi M. J. Michelbacher, Richmond, Virginia:

Sir: I have received your letter of the 15th instant, asking that furloughs may be granted to the Israelites in the army from September 30 to October 11, to enable them to repair to Richmond to observe the holy days appointed by the Jewish religion.

It would afford me much pleasure to comply with your request did the interests of the service permit it, but it is impossible to grant a general furlough to one class of our soldiers without recognizing the claims of others to a like indulgence. I can only grant furloughs on applications setting forth special grounds for them, or in accordance with the general orders on that subject applicable to all the army alike.

I will gladly do all in my power to facilitate the observance of the duties of their religion by the Israelites in the army, and I will allow them every indulgence consistent with safety and discipline. If their applications be forwarded to me in the usual way, and it appears that they can be spared, I will be glad to approve as many of them as circumstances will permit.[219]

A KNEELING CHRISTIAN

Blessing at the Table

General William Nelson Pendleton was Lee's chief of artillery. He was educated at West Point. He was also a clergyman of the Episcopal Church, and rector of Grace Church, Lexington, Virginia, both before and after the war. Among General Pendleton's private papers there was found, after his death, a correspondence relating to the dining at General Lee's headquarters. It is a touchingly intimate expression of the spirit of Christian faith and humility which animated them.

General Pendleton wrote on Wednesday, October 19, 1864, from "Headquarters Artillery Corps":

"*My dear General:* I have been so disturbed by an omission which occurred when I had the privilege of dining with you day before yesterday that I feel bound to write a brief note of apology, if it were, as is not unlikely, a misunderstanding of my own. It was the failure on my part to ask a blessing at the table. I expected to do so, and awaited your request to that effect, but did not notice one by sign or word. I may, however, have overlooked such intimation from you, or you may have taken for granted I would without it say grace. Or you may have for the time forgotten my sacred office under the military relations in which we commonly meet. In such case, however, you would, I suppose, have officiated yourself. At any rate, there was, I infer, some misunderstanding; and although not one of the more important matters of life, I would not have it pass on my own part unexplained.

"Let me also for once take occasion so far to lay aside the restraints of military etiquette as to assure you of the sincere personal friendship which I feel for yourself, and the fervent prayer with which I more than daily commend you to God's gracious guidance and blessing."

General Lee replied on Friday, October 21, 1864, from "Chaffin's," his headquarters:

My dear General: I have received your note of the 19th. I had expected you to ask a blessing on our table, and turned to you with that view. It was my fault, I think, in not making a more pointed request, which I should have done. Finding you apparently preparing to take your seat I failed to request your office, and, as is very frequently the case with me at our informal camp meals, offered a silent petition of thanks.

I reciprocate in the fullest manner your feelings of friendship, which has always been to me a source of pleasure, and am deeply obliged to you for your fervent, pious prayers in my behalf. No one stands in greater need of them. My feeble petitions I dare hardly hope will be answered.[220]

A KNEELING CHRISTIAN 147

Daily Prayer

Early in January, 1865, he wrote to his wife, closing as follows:

I pray daily and almost hourly to our Heavenly Father to come to the relief of you and our afflicted country. I know He will order all things for our good, and we must be content.[221]

Commander-in-Chief

Lee was made Commander-in-Chief of all the military forces in the Confederate States on Monday, February 6, 1865. In his order issued on accepting the command, he said:

Deeply impressed with the difficulties and responsibilities of the position, and humbly invoking the guidance of Almighty God, I rely for success upon the courage and fortitude of the army, sustained by the patriotism and firmness of the people, confident that their united efforts under the blessing of Heaven will secure peace and independence.[222]

Battle Not Always to the Strong

Thursday, February 23, 1865, he wrote to his wife in Richmond:

I think General Grant will move against us soon —within a week, if nothing prevents—and no man can tell what may be the result; but trusting to a merciful God, who does not always give the battle to the strong, I pray we may not be overwhelmed.

148 ROBERT E. LEE THE CHRISTIAN

I shall, however, endeavor to do my duty and fight to the last. Should it be necessary to abandon our position to prevent being surrounded, what will you do? You must consider the question and make up your mind. It is a fearful condition, and we must rely for guidance and protection upon a kind Providence.[223]

Joined in Prayer

When the lines had been broken below Pittsburg, Virginia, in April, 1865, General Lee went with General John B. Gordon and others into a chapel and joined heartily in a service of earnest prayer.[224]

Lee's Gethsemane

Petersburg had fallen. President Davis had made his escape from Richmond. Lee's army was surrounded, resources depleted, supplies exhausted.

"As they marched along, Lee riding Traveller, he pondered earnestly. They saw his lips move and knew that he was talking with his best Friend.

"What should he do? 'Is His mercy clean gone forever?' Had the 'Friend that sticketh closer than a brother' failed, and forsaken him after all? Had He not promised Joshua in the wilderness, 'As I was with Moses, so I will

1865] [Age 58

be with thee; I will not fail thee nor forsake thee'?

"The white, sad face seemed unconscious of those near him.

"'How easily I could get rid of this and be at rest!' he had said. 'I have only to ride along the line and all would be over. But *it is our duty to live*. What will become of the women and children of the South if we are not here to protect them?'

"He thought of the humiliation, of the pride of family, of the state, of the whole South. It had done all that it could—and lost—*failed*!"[225]

"We have appealed to the God of battles," said he, "and He has decided against us." And, now, "Lord, what wilt Thou have me to do?"

CHAPTER XV

GREAT IN DEFEAT

"Is It Right?"

ON Palm Sunday, April 9, 1865, when he had decided to see General Grant about surrendering, Lee said, "There is nothing left me but to go to General Grant, and I would rather die a thousand deaths."

A member of his staff exclaimed, "Oh, General, what will history say of the surrender of the army in the field?"

He replied:

Yes, I know they will say hard things of us; they will not understand how we were overwhelmed by numbers, but that is not the question, Colonel; the question is, Is it right to surrender this army? If it is right, then I will take all the responsibility.[226]

Colonel Archer Anderson, in an address at the unveiling of the Lee monument in Richmond, Sunday, May 29, 1890, declared:

"In those last solemn scenes, when strong men, losing all self-control, broke down and sobbed like children, Lee stood forth as great as in the days of victory and triumph. —No disaster crushed his spirit, no extremity of danger ruffled his bearing. In the agony of dissolution now invading that proud army, which for four years had wrested victory from every peril, in that blackness of utter darkness, he preserved the serene lucidity of his mind. He looked the stubborn facts calmly in the face, and when no military resource remained, when he recognized the impossibility of making another march or fighting another battle, he bowed his head in submission to that Power which makes and unmakes nations."[227]

Decision to Surrender

General E. P. Alexander remonstrated with General Lee against the surrender of the army and counseled a dispersion of the soldiers individually to rally subsequently as best they might for further resistance; and he has recorded General Lee's reply:

General, you and I as Christian men have no right to consider only how this would affect us. We must consider its effect on the country as a whole. Already it is demoralized by the four years of war. If I took your advice, the men would be without rations and under no control of officers. They would become mere bands of marauders and the enemy's cavalry would pursue them and overrun many wide sections. . . . We would bring on a state of affairs it would take the country years to recover from.[228]

Will Not Sacrifice His Men

It was the same spirit of self-denial for the good of others which he exhibited soon after his West Virginia campaign, when the newspapers and many of the people were severely criticizing him for not fighting General Rosecrans. He said to an intimate friend:

I could have fought, and I am satisfied that I could have gained a victory. But the nature of the country was such that it would have proved a barren victory, and I had rather sacrifice my military reputation and quietly rest under this unjust censure than to sacrifice unnecessarily the life of a single one of my men.[229]

Great in Defeat

Coming forth from the chamber where he signed the articles of capitulation (Appomattox, Sunday, April 9, 1865), "As he rode quietly down the lane [the Valley of Humiliation] leading from the scene of capitulation, he passed into view of his men—of such as remained of them. The news of the surrender had got abroad, and they were waiting, grief-stricken, and dejected upon the hillsides, when they caught sight of their old commander on the

GREAT IN DEFEAT 153

gray horse. Then occurred one of the most notable scenes in the history of the war.- In an instant they were about him, bareheaded, with tear-wet faces; thronging him, kissing his hand, his boots, his saddle; weeping; cheering him amid their tears; shouting his name to the very skies."[230]

He said, "Men, we have fought through the war together; I have done my best for you; my heart is too full to say more."[231]

The General then, with head bare, and tears flowing freely down his cheeks, bade adieu to the army. To one of his officers, who expressed sympathy, he said, *"Human Virtue Should be Equal to Human Calamity."*[232]

General J. A. Early, in an address before Washington and Lee University, at Lexington, Virginia, Monday, January 19, 1872, on General Lee's birthday, said, "The sword of Robert E. Lee, without a blemish on it, was sheathed forever."[233]

What Lincoln Would Do

While negotiations for the surrender were in progress, the Union commander was in touch with President Lincoln. One of the Union officers asked Lincoln what "he should do in regard to the conquered people." It is reported that Lincoln replied that he did not

1865] [Age 58

wish to give any orders on that subject, but added, "If I were in your place, I'd let 'em up easy, I'd let 'em up easy."[234]

Last Order to the Army

After General Lee returned to headquarters he issued his farewell address, the last order published to the army, "a touching memento of that sad day at Appomattox Court House," Monday, April 10, 1865:

> Headquarters Army Northern Virginia,
> April 10, 1865.

After four years of arduous service, marked by unsurpassed courage and fortitude, the Army of Northern Virginia has been compelled to yield to overwhelming numbers and resources. I need not tell the survivors of so many hard-fought battles, who have remained steadfast to the last, that I have consented to this result from no distrust of them; but, feeling that valor and devotion could accomplish nothing that could compensate for the loss that would have attended the continuation of the contest, I have determined to avoid the useless sacrifice of those whose past services have endeared them to their countrymen. By the terms of the agreement, officers and men can return to their homes and remain there until exchanged.

You will take with you the satisfaction that proceeds from the consciousness of duty faithfully performed; and I earnestly pray that a merciful

GREAT IN DEFEAT

God will extend to you his blessing and protection. With an unceasing admiration of your constancy and devotion to your country, and a grateful remembrance of your kind and generous consideration of myself, I bid you an affectionate farewell.

        (Signed)   R. E. LEE, *General*.[235]

HIS RETURN HOME

After this valedictory, Robert E. Lee, a private citizen, turned and rode away toward Richmond and his family, arriving there, Saturday, April 15, 1865. After forty years of soldier life, he was now, for the first time during his manhood, a private citizen.

President Lincoln died that morning from an assassin's bullet. The next day, Easter, General Lee attended service with his family in Saint Paul's Church.

ASSASSINATION OF LINCOLN

On Monday, September 4, 1865, General Lee wrote to the Count Joannes:

In your letter to me you do the people of the South but simple justice in believing that they heartily concur with you in opinion in regard to the assassination of the late President Lincoln. It is a crime previously unknown to this country, and one that must be deprecated by every American.[236]

CHRISTIAN CHARITY

In June, 1865, the United States Grand Jury

in Norfolk, Virginia, indicted General Lee and others for treason.

A party of friends were spending an evening at his house in Richmond, and the conversation naturally turned on these matters. The Rev. Doctor —— led the conversation in expressing, in terms of decided bitterness, the indignation of the South at the indictment of General Lee. The General pleasantly remarked,

"Well! it matters little what they may do to me; I am old, and have but a short time to live anyhow," and very soon turned the conversation into other channels.

Presently Doctor —— got up to go, and General Lee followed him out to the door and said to him very earnestly:

Doctor, there is a good old Book which I read and you preach from, which says, "Love your enemies, bless them that curse you, do good to them that hate you, and pray for them which despitefully use you and persecute you." Do you think your remarks this evening were quite in the spirit of that teaching?

Doctor —— made some apology for the bitterness which he felt and expressed, and General Lee added, with a peculiar sweetness of tone and manner that we remember so well:

I have fought against the people of the North because I believed they were seeking to wrest from the South dearest rights. But I have never cherished toward them bitter or vindictive feelings, and have never seen the day when I did not pray for them.[237]

"It is related that one day during the war, as they were reconnoitering the countless hosts opposed to them, one of his subordinates exclaimed in bitter tones, 'I wish those people were all dead!' General Lee, with that inimitable grace of manner peculiar to him, promptly rejoined: 'How can you say so, General? Now, I wish that they were all at home attending to their own business and leaving us to do the same.'"[238]

General Lee met the final test of a true Christian, the "utter and complete forgiveness of those who have injured or are trying to injure us, not the forgiveness of the lips, but the forgiveness of broad tolerance, of perfect understanding and sympathy, that is, love."

SAINT PAUL'S CHURCH, RICHMOND, VIRGINIA

Robert E. Lee and his family attended Saint Paul's Episcopal Church in Richmond.

Among the memorial windows in the church are two to General Robert E. Lee—"In Grateful Memory of Robert Edward Lee, Born January 19, 1807." One of them represents Moses leaving Pharaoh's court to join his lot with his own

158 ROBERT E. LEE THE CHRISTIAN

oppressed people, with the scriptural text bearing thereon—"By Faith Moses refused to be called the Son of Pharaoh's Daughter, choosing rather to suffer affliction with the children of God, as seeing Him who is invisible."

Regular Attendant at Country Churches

The latter part of June, 1865, General Lee and his family moved to a small cottage in the country, near Cartersville, Cumberland County, Virginia. There he spent several months of quiet and rest.

Captain Edmund Randolph Cocke wrote that "During that summer he was a regular attendant at the various churches in our neighborhood, whenever there was service."[239]

Monument at Grave of Daughter

From Rockbridge Baths, Virginia, Tuesday, July 25, 1865, in response to an invitation to be present at the unveiling of a monument at the grave of their daughter, at White Sulphur Springs, Warren County, North Carolina, he said:

My gratitude for your attention and consideration will continue through life, and my prayers will be daily offered to the throne of the Most High for his boundless blessings upon you.[240]

CHAPTER XVI

A CHRISTIAN COLLEGE PRESIDENT

ELECTED PRESIDENT OF WASHINGTON COLLEGE

FRIDAY, August 4, 1865, General Lee was elected by the board of trustees to the presidency of Washington College, at Lexington, Virginia. Before deciding to accept, he rode to the home of a friend for counsel. This friend, Bishop Joseph P. Wilmer, of Louisiana, said in an address on the occasion of General Lee's death, at the University of the South, Sewanee, Tennessee:

"I was seated," said Bishop Wilmer, "at the close of the day, in my Virginia home, when I beheld, through the thickening shades of evening, a horseman entering the yard, whom I soon recognized as General Lee. The next morning he placed in my hands the correspondence with the authorities of Washington College at Lexington. He had been invited to become president of that institution. I confess to a momentary feeling of chagrin at the proposed change (shall I say revulsion?) in his history. The institution was one of local interest, and comparatively unknown to our people. I named others more conspicuous which would welcome him with ardor as their presiding head.

"I soon discovered that his mind towered above these earthly distinctions; that, in his judgment, the *cause* gave dignity to the institution and not the wealth of its endowment, or the renown of its scholars; that this door and not another was opened to him by Providence; and he only wished to be assured of his competency to fulfill the trust, and thus to make his few remaining years a comfort and blessing to his suffering country.

"I had spoken to his human feelings; he had now revealed himself to me as one 'whose life was hid with Christ in God.' My speech was no longer restrained. I congratulated him that his heart was inclined to this great cause, and that he was spared to give to the world this august testimony to the importance of Christian education. How he listened to my feeble words; how he beckoned me to his side, as the fullness of heart found utterance; how his whole countenance glowed with animation as I spoke of the Holy Ghost as the great Teacher, whose presence was required to make education a blessing, which otherwise might be the curse of mankind; how feelingly he responded, how eloquently, as I never heard him speak before—can never be effaced from memory; and nothing more

ROBERT E. LEE
Famous painting by Mrs. H. K. Bush-Brown, of Washington, D. C. Owned by the Blue Ridge Association and hangs in Lee Hall, Blue Ridge, North Carolina.
(By permission of Dr. W. D. Weatherford, Executive Secretary.)

ROBERT E. LEE MEMORIAL CHAPEL
Exterior View
Washington and Lee University, Lexington, Virginia

ROBERT E. LEE MEMORIAL CHAPEL
Interior View
Showing recumbent statue of Lee in room back of pulpit

GRACE EPISCOPAL CHURCH
Lexington, Virginia

General Lee was a member of this church while president of Washington College. He was a member of the Vestry. His "Last Public Act" was here. (This is a new building—not the one that General Lee worshiped in.) [See page 225]

ROBERT E. LEE
on
"Traveller"
His famous war horse

A CHRISTIAN COLLEGE PRESIDENT 161

sacred mingles with my reminiscences of the dead."[241]

THE RIDE TO LEXINGTON

On Friday, September 15, 1865, General Lee mounted Traveller and rode alone to Lexington, about forty miles. He arrived on Monday, September 18. The next morning, before breakfast, he wrote to his wife, saying:

I had a very pleasant journey here. The first two days were very hot, but reaching the third day, the temperature was much cooler. I came up in four days' easy rides, getting to my stopping-place by one P. M. each day, except the third [Sunday], when I slept on top of the Blue Ridge, which I reached at three P. M. The scenery was beautiful all the way.[242]

"RIDE ON ALONE"

"Ah! ride on alone, old man, with Duty at thy bridlebit; behind thee is the glory of thy military career; before thee is the transcendent fame of thy future. Thou shalt abide there henceforth; there shall thy ashes repose; but thou shalt make of that little town a shrine to which pilgrims shall turn with softened eyes so long as men admire virtue and the heart aspires to the ideal of Duty."[243]

THE COLLEGE PRESIDENT

On Monday, October 2, 1865, "after solemn

and appropriate prayer by the Rev. W. S. White, D.D., the oldest Christian minister in the town," Lee was inaugurated president of Washington College. His salary was to be fifteen hundred dollars—"offered purely on a basis of faith!" He began his labors with this declaration:

> I have a self-imposed task which I must accomplish. I have led the young men of the South in battle; I have seen many of them fall under my standard. I shall devote my life now to training young men to do their duty in life.[244]

The preceding year the number of students had varied from thirty to forty-five. College opened September 15, 1865, with twenty-two students.[245]

The Keynote of His Life

His son Robert said, "His idea of life was to do his duty, at whatever cost, and to try to help others do theirs."[246]

Life Gliding Away

In a letter to his wife, Monday, October 9, 1865, he said:

> Life is indeed gliding away, and I have nothing of good to show for mine that is past. I pray I may be spared to accomplish something for the benefit of mankind and the honor of God.[247]

1865] [Age 58

A CHRISTIAN COLLEGE PRESIDENT 163

REASON FOR ACCEPTING PRESIDENCY

The reason for which General Lee entered upon this new work and established a new home in this mountain town, forty miles from a railroad, may be gathered from the following extract from a letter to his son, Monday, October 30, 1865:

I accepted the presidency of the college in the hope that I might be of some service to the country, and the rising generation, and not from any preference of my own. I should have selected a more quiet life and a more retired abode than Lexington and should have preferred a small farm where I could have earned my daily bread. If I find I can accomplish no good here, I will endeavor to pursue the course to which my inclinations point.[248]

HIS IDEAL OF EDUCATION

He thought it to be the office of a college not merely to educate the intellect, but to make *Christian men*. The moral and religious character of the students was even more precious in his eyes than their intellectual progress and was made the special object of his constant personal solicitude. In his annual reports to the trustees, which were models of clear and dignified composition, he always dwelt with peculiar emphasis upon these interests, and nothing in the college gratified him more than its marked moral and religious improvement during his administration.[249]

The Rev. W. S. White, D.D., the venerable pastor of the Lexington Presbyterian Church, of which General "Stonewall" Jackson was a member, states that, after a casual conversation with him one morning, he paused in parting, and was silent for a moment or two, and then said, with moistened eyes and a very earnest manner:

I shall be disappointed, sir; I shall fail in the leading object that brought me here, unless these young men all become real Christians; and I wish you, and others of your sacred profession to do all you can to accomplish this.[250]

Upon another occasion he made the same remark to the Rev. Dr. William Brown, editor of the *Central Presbyterian*, a trustee of the college, in a form more emphatic: "I dread the thought of any student going away from the college without becoming a sincere Christian."[251] The Rev. W. Strother Jones, Saint Thomas Church, New York City, who attended Washington College while General Lee was president, said:

"On one occasion, I was told that the General was noticed as deeply affected on coming out from prayers in the chapel. Someone ventured to ask, 'What is the matter, General?' To

A CHRISTIAN COLLEGE PRESIDENT 165

which he replied, 'I was thinking of my responsibility to Almighty God for these hundreds of young men.' "[252]

LEAVE RESULTS TO GOD

One day in 1866, Chaplain J. William Jones was talking to General Lee in reference to certain results of the war, when he said, very emphatically:

Yes! All that is very sad, and might be a cause of self-reproach, but that we are conscious that we have humbly tried to do our duty. We may, therefore, with calm satisfaction, trust in God and leave results to him.[253]

GIFT OF BIBLE

That Lee's Christian character was highly regarded in England is evidenced by the fact that several English admirers sent him a handsome copy of the Bible, through the Honorable A. W. Beresford Hope. The dedication reads: "General Robert E. Lee, Commanding the Confederate Army, from the Undersigned Englishmen and Englishwomen, recognizing the Genius of the General, admiring the Humanity of the Man, respecting the Virtues of the Christian."[254]

He wrote a letter of acknowledgment, Monday, April 16, 1866, in which he refers to the

Bible as "a book in comparison with which all others in my eyes are of minor importance; and which in all my perplexities has never failed to give me light and strength."[255]

Once Lee remarked to Chaplain Jones,

There are things in the old Book which I may not be able to explain, but I fully accept it as the infallible Word of God, and receive its teachings as inspired by the Holy Spirit.[256]

CHAPTER XVII

THE COLLEGE CHAPEL

When Lee became President of Washington College, his son Robert says, he urged the erection as soon as possible of a chapel, which should be of dimensions suitable for the demands of the college. There were other objects calling for a greater outlay of money than the resources of the college afforded, but he deemed this of great importance, and succeeded in getting appropriations for it first. He hastened the selection of the site and the drawing of the plans. The completion of the work was much retarded owing to the want of funds, but his interest in its erection never flagged. He gave his personal superintendence from first to last, visiting it often two or three times a day. (This building is now known as the "Lee Memorial Chapel.")

After it was dedicated (1867) he always attended morning prayers and all other religious exercises held there, unless prevented by sickness. His son Robert says: "Whenever I was there on a visit, I always went with him every morning to chapel. He had a certain seat which he occupied, and you could have kept your watch regulated by the time he entered the doors. As he thought well of the young men who left his drawing room by ten o'clock, so he placed in a higher estimate those who attended chapel regularly, especially if they got there in proper time."

There was no regular chaplain, but the ministers of the different denominations who had churches in the village undertook, by turns, to perform a month's service.[257]

To His Son Robert Edward, Jr.

Writing to his son, Robert E. Lee, Jr., Saturday, May 26, 1866, concerning the farm he had received by his grandfather's will, General Lee said:

I wish, my dear son, I could be of some advantage to you, but I can only give you my love and earnest prayer, and commit you to the keeping of that God who never forgets those who serve Him. May He watch over and preserve you.[258]

Stolen Bible

Writing from Lexington, to the Honorable A. J. Requier, New York, Wednesday, September 5, 1866, Lee said:

So many articles formerly belonging to me are scattered over the country that I fear I have not time to devote to their recovery. I know no one in

THE COLLEGE CHAPEL 169

Buffalo whom I could ask to reclaim the Bible in question. If the lady who has it will use it, as I hope she will, she will herself seek to restore it to its rightful owner.[259]

REFUSES GIFT OF HAT

A firm in Baltimore offered to send him a hat. He replied from Lexington, June 1, 1866:

I am much obliged to you for your kind offer to send me a hat, and I appreciate most highly the motives which prompted it. When so many are destitute, I dislike to have more than I actually require, and yet am unwilling to appear insensible to your sentiments of friendship and sympathy. I have a very good hat, which will answer my purpose the whole year, and I would, therefore, prefer that you would give to others what I really do not require. If, however, after what I have said, you still wish to present me with what I can well do without, I cannot refuse what you say will be a gratification to you.[260]

ACCEPTS CHAPEL BIBLE

Colonel F. R. Farrar, a gallant Confederate soldier and widely known lecturer, sent General Lee a copy of the Bible for the pulpit in the college chapel. Following is the brief letter of acceptance, beautiful and comprehensive in its diction, Thursday, September 19, 1867:

I beg you will accept my sincere thanks for the

beautiful Bible which you have presented to me—a book which supplies the place of all others, and one that cannot be replaced by any other. I will place it in the chapel of Washington College, as you desire, where I trust its simple truths will be daily learned and thoroughly appreciated by all the students.[261]

Chapel Services

The following letter, which is only one of several of the same import, exhibits his views on religious services, and his broad spirit, written Wednesday, September 11, 1869:

Reverend and Dear Sirs: Desirous of making the religious exercises of the college advantageous to the students, and wishing to use all means to inculcate among them the principles of true religion, the Faculty tender to you their cordial thanks for your past services, and request you to perform in rotation the customary daily exercises at the college chapel. The hour fixed for these services is forty-five minutes past seven o'clock every morning, except Sunday, during the session, save the three winter months, December, January, and February, when the hour for prayer will be forty-five minutes past eight. The hours for lectures are fixed at eight and nine o'clock respectively during these periods. On Sundays the hour for prayer during the whole session is fixed at nine o'clock.

The Faculty also request that you will extend to the students a general invitation to attend the

churches of their choice regularly on Sundays and
other days; and invite them to join the Bible classes
established in each; that you will, as may be convenient and necessary, visit them in sickness and in
health; and that you will in every proper manner
urge upon them the great importance of the Christian religion.

The Faculty further asks that you will arrange
among yourselves, as may be most convenient, the
periods of the session during which each will perform chapel services, and that during those periods
the officiating minister will consider himself chaplain of the college, for the purpose of conducting
religious worship, prayers, etc.

The present session will open on the 16th instant
and close on the 25th of June, 1870.

I am, with great respect, your obedient servant,

R. E. LEE.

To the ministers of the Baptist, Episcopal, Methodist, and Presbyterian Churches in Lexington,
Virginia.[262]

LIKED PRACTICAL SERMONS

Lee was not accustomed to indulge in carping
criticisms of sermons, but was a most intelligent
judge of what a sermon ought to be, and always
expressed his preference for those sermons which
presented most simply and earnestly the soul-
saving truths of the gospel. In reference to a
Baccalaureate sermon preached at the college
by the Rev. Dr. J. A. Broadus, a professor in

the Southern Baptist Theological Seminary, he said:

It was a noble sermon—one of very best I ever heard—and the beauty of it was that the preacher gave our young men the very marrow of the gospel, and with a simple earnestness that must have reached their hearts and done them good.[263]

Upon another occasion a distinguished minister had addressed the Young Men's Christian Association of the college, and on the next night delivered a popular lecture. Speaking of the latter, General Lee said:

It was a very fine lecture, and I enjoyed it. But I did not like it as much as I did the one before our Christian Association. *That* touched our hearts and did us all good.[264]

Liked Appropriate Prayers

He had also a most intelligent appreciation of the adaptation of religious services to particular occasions, and of the appropriateness of prayers to the time and place in which they were offered. He once said to one of the faculty:

I want you to go with me to call upon Mr. ——, the new minister who has just come to town. I want to pay my respects to him, and to invite him to take his turn in the conduct of our chapel exercises, and to do what he can for the spiritual interests of our young men.

And do you think that it would be any harm for me to delicately hint to Mr. —— that we would be glad if he would make his morning prayers *a little short?* You know our friend —— —— is accustomed to make his prayers too long. He prays for the Jews, the Turks, the heathen, the Chinese, and everybody else, and makes his prayers run into the regular hour for our college recitations. Would it be wrong for me to suggest to Mr. —— that he confine his morning prayers to us poor sinners at the college and pray for the Turks, the Jews, the Chinese, and the other heathen some other time?[265]

Religious Example

One striking feature of President Lee's collegiate incumbency was the religious spirit which animated the institution. His religion had a genuine catholicity of character. The dogmas of sects were less to him than the essential and universal truths of spiritual faith. He did not believe in *enforced* religion, and never required the students by any college law to attend chapel or church, but he did everything in his power to influence them to do so, and with large success.

He was a most regular attendant upon all of the services of his own church, his seat in the college chapel was never vacant unless he was kept away by sickness, and if there was a union prayer meeting, or a service of general interest in any of the churches of Lexington, General Lee was sure to be among the most devout attendants.

His pew in his own church was immediately in front of the chancel, his seat in the chapel was the second from the pulpit; he seemed always to prefer a seat near the preacher's stand. He always devoutly knelt during prayer, and his attitude during the entire service was that of an interested listener or a reverential participant.

It naturally followed that "the demeanor of the students during worship was characterized by so much decorum and evinced so deep an interest in the services as to have been the subject of frequent remarks alike by citizens and strangers—it presented so striking a contrast to what they had been accustomed to witness among the same class when under the operation of a different management."[266]

College President and a Little Child

There was a child at Lexington who was accustomed to clamber up by the side of General Lee at the college chapel exercises, and who was so kindly treated that whenever he saw his distinguished friend he straightway assumed a position beside him. At the college Commencement the little fellow glided from his mother's side and quietly stole up to the platform. Soon he was nestled at the feet of the dignified president, gazing up into his face, utterly oblivious of the crowd. Resting his head confidingly upon the knees of his chosen patron, he went fast asleep. General Lee tenderly remained without moving, preferring to suffer from the constrained position rather than disturb the sleeping child. (The child has grown up and is now a Baptist minister, the Rev. Mr. Jones.)[267]

A distinguished lady present remarked that "this picture of helpless innocence confidingly resting on greatness formed a subject worthy of the greatest artist."

CHAPTER XVIII

RELIGIOUS WELFARE OF STUDENTS

As we have indicated, Lee was greatly interested in the religious life of the young men in Washington college. The Rev. Dr. Thomas J. Kirkpatrick, professor of moral philosophy, relates the following:

"We had been conversing for some time respecting the religious welfare of the students. General Lee's feelings soon became so intense that for a time his utterance was choked; but, recovering himself, with his eyes overflowing with tears, his lips quivering with emotion, and both hands raised, he exclaimed, 'Oh, Doctor! if I could only know that all the young men in this college were good Christians, I should have nothing more to desire'!"[268]

"You will remember that this man surrendered a great army and saw a nation sink to dust without a tear."

"His devout personal piety increased with his years, and his prayers were continually offered in behalf of those committed to his charge. His fervor in the guidance of the young grew more marked."[269]

No Sunday Traveling

His interest in the moral and spiritual welfare of students can be shown by one incident in Washington College:

"Several of my friends," said Mr. David J. Wilson, "thought of making a trip to the Natural Bridge (fourteen miles away) on Sunday. It was suggested that one of our party should see General Lee the evening before, make known our intention, and secure his assent. But when the General heard of the plan he refused his assent and said it was not only against college rules to leave the town on Sunday, but it was wrong to spend Sunday in traveling for pleasure."[270]

Young Men's Christian Association

President Lee fostered the organization of a Young Men's Christian Association among the students, contributing fifty dollars a year to its fund and donating to it a specially collected library. In his reports to the Board of Trustees he gave detailed mention of this society, and dwelt upon the religious influence it exerted. Upon the matriculation of a new student, his religious faith was inquired into, and it was sought at once to bring him in close relations with the pastor of the church of his belief. Nothing better illustrated General Lee's theory of collegiate training than did this tender solicitude for the spiritual welfare and culture of his students. He had a loftier idea of education than that comprised in the laborious task of the textbook. His view of a true education embraced the moral expansion of mind and soul, the implanting of high principles of manhood, and of a delicate sense of honor; and he often expressed himself as feeling that his duty would be ill done were not his students led to become consistent Christians. His own life exemplified his teachings.[271]

HONORARY MEMBER OF YOUNG MEN'S CHRISTIAN ASSOCIATION

General Lee's letter in reply to one making him an honorary member of the association is as follows:

I have received your letter announcing my election as an honorary member of the Young Men's Christian Association of Washington College—a society in whose prosperity I take the deepest interest and for the welfare of whose members my prayers are daily offered. Please present my grateful thanks to your association for the honor conferred on me.[272]

NEW SUNDAY-SCHOOL SCHOLAR

The superintendent of one of the Sunday schools of Lexington once offered a prize to the scholar who should bring into the school by a given time the largest number of new scholars, and the pastor of the church urged that they should not confine their efforts to the children, but should seek to bring in the old as well, since none were too wise to study God's Word. A boy of five caught the spirit of the pastor's speech and went after his friend General Lee, to beg him to "go with me to our Sunday school and be my new scholar." The little fellow was greatly disappointed when told that the General attended another church, and said with a deep sigh: "I am very sorry. I wish you belonged to our church, so that you could go to our Sunday school and be my new scholar."

The General was very much amused, and kindly answered his little friend:

Ah! C——, we must all try to be *good Christians* —that is the most important thing. I can't go to your Sunday school to be your new scholar to-day. But I am very glad you asked me. It shows that you are zealous in a good cause, and I hope that you will continue to be so as you grow up.

And I do not want you to think that I consider myself too old to be a Sunday-school scholar. No one ever becomes too old to study the precious truths of the Bible.

This last remark was evidently intended for several of the college students who were near by and listening with deep interest to the colloquy between the General and the young recruiting officer of the Sunday-school army.[273]

Revivals

In 1865, after the war ended, a general revival of religion extended through Virginia. Former army chaplain J. William Jones told General Lee about it, and said that large numbers of the returned soldiers were among the converts. Tears started in his eyes, as he replied with emotion,

"I am delighted to hear that; I wish that all of them would become Christians, for it is about all that is left the poor fellows now."[274]

When Doctor Jones was starting in the spring of 1869 on a tour through several of the Southern states, General Lee said to him,

You will meet many of my old soldiers during your trip, and I wish you to tell them that I often think of them, try every day to pray for them, and am always gratified to hear of their prosperity.

As this message was repeated at different points, strong men wept as they said, "God bless the old chief; he is the noblest specimen of a man that ever lived!"[275]

Report to Board of Trustees

The following extract from General Lee's last Annual Report to the Board of Trustees, 1869]   [Age 62

RELIGIOUS WELFARE OF STUDENTS 181

June 21, 1870, is confirmation of his great interest in the religion of the students:

Prayers have been offered every morning in the college chapel by clergymen of the different denominations in Lexington, who volunteered at the beginning of the session to perform this service in rotation. The students were in this way introduced to their acquaintance, and were invited to attend the churches of their preference and to join Bible classes organized in each for their instruction. They are thus early surrounded by favorable influences, which in many cases end in the happiest results.

The Young Men's Christian Association of the college continues to prosper and is productive of much good. There are eighty-eight members of the association this year. There is an assembly for prayer every night, and a general prayer meeting once a week. A Sabbath-school house has been built near House Mountain by the association, and a Sunday school organized near Thorn Hill.

Fifty students are engaged in teaching in Sunday schools and Bible classes. There are twenty-one candidates for the ministry in the college this year, and one hundred and nine church members, nineteen of whom have joined the churches in Lexington during this session. A general and active religious feeling exists among the students, and missionary meetings are held once a month.[276]

Christian Spirit of Forgiveness

Soon after the "Reconstruction Acts" were

passed, two of the professors of the college were talking with General Lee, when one of them expressed himself in very bitter terms against the unrelenting spirit which presided over the enactment of such statutes. General Lee took from the table some manuscript pages of his father's *Life*, which he was then editing, and read these lines:

"Learn from yon Orient shell to love thy foe,
  And store with pearls the hand that brings thee
    woe:
Free, like yon rock, from base, vindictive pride,
Emblaze with gems the wrist that rends thy side.
Mark where yon tree rewards the stony shower
With fruit nectareous, or the balmy flower;
All Nature cries aloud. Shall men do less
Than love the smiter and the railer bless?"

Said he:

The lines were written in Arabia and by a Mohammedan, the poet of Shiraz, the immortal Hafiz; and ought not we, who profess to be governed by the principles of Christianity, to rise at least to the standard of this Mohammedan poet and learn to forgive our enemies?[277]

"His heart was so clean and free from any 'lurking root of bitterness' that, as he passed through the furnace of affliction, he grew more and more into the likeness of the 'Man of

RELIGIOUS WELFARE OF STUDENTS 183

Sorrows.' If ever a son of man beheld the Son of man in His truth and beauty, it was Robert Edward Lee."[278]

ABANDON ANIMOSITIES

When a lady cherished some bitterness toward the Government, General Lee said:

Madam, don't bring up your sons to detest the United States Government. Recollect that we form one country now. Abandon all these local animosities and make your sons Americans.[279]

REBUKES CRITIC OF GENERAL GRANT

One of his university faculty had been criticizing the Union general with some harshness. General Lee said, emphatically,

Sir, if you ever presume again to speak disrespectfully of General Grant in my presence, either you or I will sever his connection with this university.[280]

OMIT BITTER EXPRESSIONS

Upon the occasion of the delivery of an address at Washington College by a certain distinguished orator, General Lee went to the Rev. J. William Jones, D.D., and said:

I saw you taking notes during the address. It was in the main very fine; but, if you propose publishing any report of it, I would suggest that you leave out all the bitter expressions against the North and the United States Government. They will do no good under our present circumstances, and I think all such expressions undignified and unbecoming.[281]

"Hate dies quickest in the soldier. It is the civil population of former enemies who continue to spit fire at each other longest after hostilities have ceased. Every war has proved it, but none better than our own Civil War. And no one soldier in history ever proved it better than the South's first soldier—Robert E. Lee."[282]

Dr. J. William Jones relates the following:
"One day in the autumn of 1869, I saw General Lee standing at his gate, talking to a humbly clad man, who turned off, evidently delighted with his interview, just as I came up. After exchanging salutations, the General pleasantly said, pointing to the retreating form, 'That is one of our old soldiers who is in necessitous circumstances.' I took it for granted that it was some veteran Confederate, and asked to what command he belonged, when the General quietly and pleasantly added, 'He fought on the other side, but we must not remember that against him now.'

"The man afterward came to my house and said to me, in speaking of his interview with General Lee: 'Sir, he is the noblest man that ever lived. He not only had a kind word for an old soldier who fought against him, but he gave me some money to help me on my way.'

"What a beautiful illustration of the teaching of the apostle: ... 'If thine enemy hunger, feed him; if he thirst, give him drink'!"[283]

CHAPTER XIX

FINANCIAL TEMPTATION

AT the close of the war, offers of financial assistance poured upon him from all quarters—houses, lands, and money; but he steadfastly refused them. An English nobleman, thinking that he would rejoice in some place of retreat, wrote to offer him a splendid country-seat in England and an annuity of $15,000. His reply was simple and noble: "I am deeply grateful, but I cannot consent to desert my native state in the hour of her adversity. I must abide her fortunes and share her fate."[284]

Soon after he went to Lexington (1865), he was visited by an agent of a certain insurance company, who offered him their presidency, at a salary of $10,000 a year; he was then receiving only $3,000 from the college, the salary having been increased to that amount.

He told the agent that he could not give up the position he then held, and could not properly attend to the duties of both.

"But, General," said the agent, "we do not want you to discharge any duties. We simply want the use of your name; *that* will abundantly compensate us."

FINANCIAL TEMPTATION 187

"Excuse me, sir," was the prompt and decided rejoinder; "I cannot consent to receive pay for services I do not render."[285]

The grandeur of his character shines forth in his further reply: "My good name is about all that I have saved from the wreck of the war, and that is not for sale."[286]

General Lee received numerous letters filled with offers of remunerative positions, to which he always replied that he preferred to continue the educational work he had undertaken; but still they came coupled often with the condition that he should not relinquish his self-imposed task, and should not resign the college presidency. On one occasion the General said to a particular friend in his office:

My friend, Mr. ——, has been to see me and offers me twenty thousand dollars per annum to take the presidency of —— Company. I would like to make some money for Mrs. Lee, as she has not much left, and he does not require me to leave the college; what do you think of my accepting it?

The irony of the question was appreciated, but his friend took him at his word, and expressed his opinion adversely, saying, as modestly as possible, that if he "allowed himself to be influenced by filthy lucre he would begin to gravitate." With the winsome way so charac-

188   ROBERT E. LEE THE CHRISTIAN

teristic of him the General replied: "I am glad to find that you agree with me. I told Mr. —— yesterday that I must decline the offer."[287]

Nearly every mail brought him some such proposition, and just a short time before his death a large and wealthy corporation of New York City offered him a salary of $50,000 a year if he would consent to be their president.

In reply to this offer he wrote, "Do you not think that if my name is worth $50,000 a year, I ought to be very careful about taking care of it?"[288]

He steadfastly refused all such offers, and quietly pursued his chosen path of duty.[289]

Hon. H. W. Hilliard, ex-member of the Federal Congress, made a speech in Augusta, Georgia, at the meeting held there to do honor to the memory of General Lee, in which he said:

"An offer, originating in Georgia, and I believe in this very city, was made to him to place an immense sum of money at his disposal if he would consent to reside in the city of New York and represent Southern commerce. Millions would have flowed to him. But he declined."[290]

REFUSES OFFERS FROM BOARD OF TRUSTEES

When the Board of Trustees of Washington

College called General Lee to its presidency, they were anxious to fulfill the wishes and expectations of the Southern public by paying such salary as his wide reputation and invaluable services were entitled to receive. This feeling increased as they saw the college expand under his magic touch, until, from an institution with five professors and some sixty students, it numbered more than twenty instructors and over four hundred students. But they always found an insurmountable difficulty in the steadfast refusal of General Lee to receive a salary beyond what he conceived the funds of the institution and fairness to the other members of the Faculty would justify. It was in vain that the Faculty united with the trustees in urging that the prosperity of the college was due to his influence; that his name had secured the endowment whereby the additional professors were appointed, and had attracted young men from every state; that they were offering him no gratuity, but simply a compensation for his invaluable services. His firm reply was, "My salary is as large as the college ought to pay."[291]

The trustees were anxious to have built for him a handsome residence, and friends in different sections contributed funds for the purpose, but he insisted that other buildings were needed far more than a new house for himself. The trustees finally made the appropriation without his knowledge, and he then superintended the building himself, reduced its cost considerably below the amount appropriated, and was very careful always to speak of it not as his own (as the trustees meant it to be), but as "the president's house."

In the spring of 1870 the Board of Trustees deeded to Mrs. Lee this house and settled on her an annuity of three thousand dollars. When the General heard of it, he wrote, in Mrs. Lee's behalf, a polite but firm letter, declining the offer.

The trustees still delicately adhered to their purpose, had the deed quietly recorded, and after General Lee's death sent Mrs. Lee a check for the annuity. But this noble Virginia matron had caught the spirit of her husband, and returned the check with a beautiful letter declining to allow any of the funds of the college to be diverted to her private use, or to receive for her family any part of the property of the institution.

Refuses Benefit Fund

Certain wealthy friends and admirers of General Lee one summer, at the White Sulphur Springs, put on foot a scheme to raise $50,000

FINANCIAL TEMPTATION

which they designed to be used by the college for his benefit during his life, and to revert to his family at his death. He declined to allow this fund to be raised, except on the condition that instead of going to the benefit of his family, it should be a *permanent endowment* of the president's chair of the college.[292]

Opposed Slavery

Mr. Herbert C. Saunders, an English gentleman, had a long interview with General Lee at Lexington, in November, 1865, in which his opinions on several things are given.

"On the subject of slavery," Mr. Saunders said, "he assured me that he had always been in favor of the emancipation of the Negroes, and that in Virginia the feeling had been strongly inclining in the same direction, till the ill-judged enthusiasms (amounting to rancor) of the abolitionists in the North turned the Southern tide of feeling in the other direction. He went on to say that there was scarcely a Virginian now who was not glad that the subject had been definitely settled, though nearly all regretted that they had not been wise enough to do it themselves the first year of the war."[293]

CHAPTER XX

THE COMFORTER

LETTER TO MRS. JEFFERSON DAVIS

WRITING to the wife of President Jefferson Davis, at Prospect Hill, Georgia, Friday, February 23, 1866, from Lexington, General Lee said:

As regards the treatment of the Andersonville prisoners, to which you allude, I know nothing and can say nothing of my own knowledge. I never had anything to do with any prisoners, except to send those taken on the fields, where I was engaged, to the Provost Marshal General at Richmond.

I have felt most keenly the sufferings and imprisonment of your husband, and have earnestly consulted with friends as to any possible mode of affording him relief and consolation. He enjoys the sympathy and respect of all good men; and, if, as you state, his trial is now near, the exhibition of the whole truth in his case will, I trust, prove his defense and justification. With sincere prayers for his health and speedy restoration to liberty, and earnest supplication to God that He may take you and yours under His guidance and protection.[294]

He said, "I court the most searching investigation into this matter."[295]

THE COMFORTER

Chaplain J. William Jones said, "No man, living or dead, ever heard General Lee utter an unkind word to a prisoner, or saw him maltreat in the slightest degree, any who fell into his power."[296]

REFUTES SLANDER

Writing from Lexington, Thursday, March 1, 1866, to an old and long-tried friend, Mr. E. J. Quirk, San Francisco, California, concerning his denial of a certain slander circulated about General Lee, that he was responsible for the alleged "cruel treatment" of servants, he said, "No servant, soldier, or citizen, that was ever employed by me, can with truth charge me with bad treatment."[297]

LETTER OF COMFORT TO MRS. ELLIOTT

On the death of Bishop Stephen Elliott, of Georgia, he wrote to Mrs. Elliott, Thursday, February 21, 1867, saying:

You have my deepest sympathy, and my earnest prayers are offered to Almighty God that He may be graciously pleased to comfort you in your great sorrow, and to bring you in His own good time to rejoice with him whom in His all-wise providence He has called before you to heaven.[298]

REWARD OF THE RIGHTEOUS

In a letter to the widow of General George

W. Randolph (for a time Confederate Secretary of War), Thursday, April 11, 1867, he said:

It is the survivors of the sad event whom I commiserate, and not him whom a gracious God has called to Himself; and whose tender heart and domestic virtues make the pang of parting the more bitter to those who are left behind. I deferred writing, for I knew the hopelessness of offering you consolation; and yet for what other purpose can a righteous man be summoned into the presence of a merciful God than to receive his reward? However, then, we lament, we ought not to deplore him or wish him back from his peaceful, happy home.[299]

Death of Mrs. Hoge

In a letter to the Rev. Dr. Moses D. Hoge, the great Presbyterian preacher of Richmond, Virginia, soon after the death of his wife, after speaking of a number of matters connected with the Virginia Bible Society, he concluded as follows:

And now, my dear sir, though perhaps inappropriate to the occasion, you must allow me to refer to a subject which has caused me great distress and concerning which I have desired to write ever since its occurrence; but, to tell the truth, I have not had the heart to do so. I knew how powerless I was to give any relief and how utterly inadequate was any language that I could use even to mitigate your suffering.

I could, therefore, only offer up my silent prayers to Him who alone can heal your bleeding heart, that in His infinite mercy He would be ever present with you—to dry your tears and staunch your wounds; to sustain you by His grace and support you by His strength.

I hope you felt assured that in this heavy calamity you and your children had the heartfelt sympathy of Mrs. Lee and myself, and that you were daily remembered in our prayers.[300]

Jefferson Davis Released from Prison

When Jefferson Davis was released from the prison at Fortress Monroe, where he had been confined for about two years, General Lee wrote him the following beautiful letter from Lexington, Saturday, June 1, 1867, which gives some idea of the distress of his heart:

My dear Mr. Davis: You can conceive better than I can express the misery which your friends have suffered from your long imprisonment, and the other afflictions incident thereto. To none has this been more painful than to me, and the impossibility of affording relief has added to my distress. Your release has lifted a load from my heart which I have not words to tell, and my daily prayer to the great Ruler of the world is, that He may shield you from all future harm, guard you from all evil, and give you that peace which the world cannot take away.

1867] [Age 60

That the rest of your days may be triumphantly happy is the sincere and earnest wish of
Your most obedient, faithful friend and servant,
R. E. LEE.[301]

LONGS FOR A HOME IN A QUIET SPOT

In a letter to his son Fitzhugh, Saturday, June 8, 1867, he said:

I, therefore, can anticipate for you many years of happiness and prosperity, and in my daily prayers to the God of mercy and truth I invoke His choicest blessings upon you. May He gather you under the shadow of His almighty wing, direct you in all your ways, and give you peace and everlasting life. It would be most pleasant to my feelings could I again, as you propose, gather you all around me, but I fear that will not be in this world. Let us all so live that we may be united in that world where there is no more separation, and where sorrow and pain never come.

I think after next year I will have done all the good I can for the college, and I should then like, if peace is restored to the country, to retire to some quiet spot, east of the mountains, where I might prepare a home for your mother and sisters after my death, and where I could earn my daily bread.[302]

TO MISS ANN UPSHUR JONES

General Lee wrote of Washington College to Miss Ann Upshur Jones, Brooklyn, New York, Monday, June 24, 1867,

THE COMFORTER

Located in a Presbyterian community, it is natural that the most of its trustees and faculty should be of that denomination, though the rector, president, and several of the professors are members of the Episcopal Church.[303]

Another letter to Miss Jones, thanking her for a donation to the college, closed with, "Praying that the great and merciful God may throw around you His protecting care and love."[304]

TO DAUGHTER ON THE DEATH OF HER FATHER

Writing from Lexington, Friday, July 5, 1867, to Miss Josephine Seaton, Baltimore, Maryland, he closed:

You have my sincere sympathy in this afflicting event, and my prayers to Him who cares for the fatherless, that He may guide and protect you.[305]

TO HIS NEW DAUGHTER-IN-LAW

Tuesday, March 10, 1868, he wrote to his new daughter-in-law, Fitzhugh's second wife:

I hope everything is agreeable, and that you are becoming more and more interested in making those around you happy. That is the true way to secure your own happiness, for which my poor prayers are daily offered to the throne of the Most High.[306]

ATTENDS SAINT PAUL'S CHURCH, BALTIMORE

In April, 1869, being in Baltimore on business,

Sunday intervening, he attended service in the morning at Saint Paul's Church on Charles Street. When it became known that General Lee was there, large numbers collected to see him come out, waiting patiently and quietly until the congregation was dismissed. As he appeared at the door all heads were uncovered and kept so until he had passed through the long line extending down the street.[307]

To Father on Accidental Death of Son

In a letter to a father, regarding the accidental death of his son at college, he said:

When one, in the pureness and freshness of youth, before having been contaminated by sin or afflicted by misery, is called to the presence of his Merciful Creator, it must be solely for his good. As difficult as this may be for you now to recognize, I hope you will keep it constantly in your memory and take it to your comfort; and I pray that He who in His wise Providence has permitted this crushing sorrow may sanctify it to the happiness of all.[308]

To Mother on Accidental Death of Son

In a letter, Sunday, April 6, 1868, to the mother of a student at the college, who had been drowned, his closing words were:

May God in His mercy support you under this grievous trial and give you that peace which, as it

THE COMFORTER

passeth all understanding, so nothing in this world can diminish or destroy it.[309]

Visit of Bishop Whipple

Tuesday, May 11, 1869, in a letter to his son, Fitzhugh, he said:

Bishop Whipple [Episcopal] will be here Friday next and is invited to stay with us. There are to be a great many preparatory religious exercises this week. A great feeling of religion pervades the young in the community, especially at the Virginia Military Institute.[310]

Comfort in Sorrow

The following brief letter was written to Mr. Samuel R. George, Baltimore, Maryland, on Monday, February 28, 1870, from Lexington, Virginia:

I have learned with deep regret the great sorrow that has befallen you, and sincerely sympathize in your overwhelming grief. But the great God of heaven takes us at the period when it is best for us to go, and we can only gratefully acknowledge His mercy and try to be resigned to His will. Every beat of our hearts marks our progress through life and admonishes us of the steps we make towards the grave. We are thus every moment reminded to prepare for our summons.[311]

CHAPTER XXI

GENERAL LEE AND TEMPERANCE

FRIENDS OF TEMPERANCE

THAT he felt a lively interest in promoting sobriety among the young men of the college, the following letter will show, written on Thursday, December 9, 1869:

Messrs. S. G. M. Miller, J. L. Logan, T. A. Ashby,
    Committee.

Gentlemen:

The announcement, in your letter of the 8th instant, of an organization of the "Friends of Temperance" in the college has given me great gratification. I sincerely hope that it may be the cause of lasting good, not only to the members themselves, but to all those with whom they associate to the extent of their influence and example. My experience through life has convinced me that, while moderation and temperance in all things are commendable and beneficial, abstinence from spirituous liquors is the best safeguard to morals and health. The evidence on this subject that has come within my own observation is conclusive to my mind, and, without going into the recital, I cannot too earnestly exhort you to practice habitual temperance, so that you may form the habit in youth, and not feel the inclination, or temptation, to depart from

GENERAL LEE AND TEMPERANCE 201

it in manhood. By so doing your health will be maintained, your morals elevated, and your success in life promoted. I shall at all times, and in whatever way I can, take great pleasure in advancing the object of your society, and you may rely on my co-operation in the important work in which you have engaged.[312]

Close Grog-Shops

Chaplain J. William Jones says that he was walking with General Lee one day in Lexington, during the sway of the military, when, seeing a young man stagger out of one of the barrooms, the General, who seemed very much annoyed by the spectacle, said:

I wish that these military gentlemen, while they are doing so many things which they have no right to do, would close up all of these grog-shops which are luring our young men to destruction.[313]

"He rarely took even a glass of wine. Whisky or brandy he did not drink, and he did all in his power to discourage their use in others."[314]

His wife said that when he returned from the Mexican War, he brought back "a bottle of brandy which he had taken in case of sickness, *unopened.*"[315]

Carried Brandy Through the War

In the spring of 1861, while on an inspection

tour to Norfolk, Virginia, a friend there insisted that he should take two bottles of very fine old "London Dock" brandy, remarking that he would be certain to need it, and would find it very difficult to obtain so good an article. General Lee declined the offer, saying that he was sure he would not need it. He said:

As proof that I will not, I may tell you that, just as I was starting to the Mexican War, a lady in Virginia prevailed on me to take a bottle of fine old whisky, which she thought I could not get on without. I carried that bottle all through the war without having had the slightest occasion to use it, and on my return home I sent it back to my good friend, that she might be convinced that I could get on without liquor.

But the gentleman still insisted, and the General politely yielded and took two bottles.

At the close of the war he met a brother of this gentleman, who told this incident, in Lexington, and said to him:

Tell your brother that I kept the brandy he gave me all through the war, and should have it yet, but that I was obliged to use it last summer in a severe illness of one of my daughters.[316]

During the war he was accustomed to do everything in his power, both by precept and example, to prevent drunkenness among his officers and men, and more than once he refused to promote an officer who drank too freely, saying, "I cannot consent to place in control of others one who cannot control himself."[317]

Tobacco

"Throughout his whole life, he never used tobacco," and he tried to keep his boys from using it.[318]

The Rev. Edward Clifford Gordon, officially connected with Washington College when Lee was president, said, "He did not use tobacco in any form."[319]

Losing His Temper

Colonel A. L. Long, his military secretary, speaks of "General Lee's losing his temper—a circumstance which happened only twice, to my knowledge, during my long acquaintance with him. He was not wanting in temper, but was, on the contrary, a man of decided character and strong passions; yet he had such complete control of himself that few men ever knew him to deviate from his habitual calm dignity of mien."[320]

One of the times when he became angry was when "He paused amid the pressing duties at Gettysburg to reprove an officer who was beating an unruly horse."[321]

Profanity

His most intimate friends never heard him utter an oath.[322]

Clean in Speech

One who knew him from his boyhood to his grave declared that he never knew him "to utter an immoral or profane word."

"He never used slang nor told a joke which his wife and daughters might not have listened to with perfect propriety."[323]

A member of a church (not his own), who had known him intimately for years, said that "his lips were never soiled by a profane or obscene word, and that when the provocation was great for a display of angry feelings, it was his course to use the 'soft answer which turneth away wrath.' "[324]

CHAPTER XXII

A MAN OF PRAYER

A MAN of prayer, he had his regular hours of secret devotion which he allowed nothing else, however pressing, to interrupt. He neglected no opportunity of joining in the public devotions of God's people. Chaplain Jones said:

"I saw him frequently at our services in the army, as he listened with moistened eyes to the truths of the gospel, or bowed in the dust as some one led the devotions of the congregation. How vividly I recall those scenes at 'Stonewall' Jackson's headquarters when thousands of the men in gray would assemble for worship and the ragged jacket of the men of the ranks would mingle with 'the bars,' 'the stars,' and 'the wreaths' of rank. Among the most notable, but most devout, of the officers were Jackson and his beloved commander, R. E. Lee."[325]

FAMILY PRAYERS

General Lee always had his family altar and read family prayers every morning just before breakfast. A daughter-in-law, after her first visit to General Lee, spending three weeks there, said that she did not believe he would have an entirely high opinion of any person, even General Washington, if he could return to earth, if he were not in time for family prayers.[326]

The Rev. Dr. W. T. Brantly, a Baptist minister, said:

"When a guest at his house, the first thing with which he greeted me, on coming down in the morning, was the Bible, with a request that I should lead the devotions of the family; and when, after reading God's Word, we knelt down together, his prompt and cordial responses attested the earnestness with which he adopted the petitions addressed to the Throne of Grace."[327]

One of his sons said that "family prayers ... were read every morning just before breakfast," which was served at seven o'clock, and another son warned his wife that "to please father, she must be always ready for family prayers."[328]

Concert of Prayer for Colleges

"At the 'Concert of Prayer for Colleges,' in Lexington, in 1869," says Chaplain J. William Jones, "I made an address in which I urged that the great need of our colleges was a genuine, pervasive revival—that this could only come from God; and that inasmuch as He has promised His Holy Spirit to those who ask Him, we should make special prayer for a revival in the colleges of the country, and more particularly in Washington College and the Virginia Military Institute. At the close of the meeting General Lee came to me and said, with more than his usual warmth:

I wish, sir, to thank you for your address; it was just what we needed. Our great want is a revival which shall bring these young men to Christ.

We poor sinners need to come back from our wanderings to seek pardon through the all-sufficient merits of our Redeemer. And we need to pray earnestly for the power of the Holy Spirit to give us a precious revival in our hearts and among the unconverted."[329]

Realization of God's Mercy

"Upon several other occasions," says Chaplain Jones, "I heard him express himself in similar terms, and have never known a man who more carefully realized that he was 'a sinner saved by grace,' a sinner cleansed in the atoning blood of Christ, a sinner whose only hope of salvation was built on 'the Rock of Ages.'"

During the great revival which followed in the Virginia Military Institute, also located in Lexington, in 1869, in which one hundred ten cadets professed conversion, he said to his pastor, with deep emotion:

I rejoice to hear that. It is the best news I have heard since I have been in Lexington. Would that we could have such a revival in all our colleges![330]

Delegate to Episcopal Council

Since he had lived in Lexington, General Lee had been a member of the vestry of Grace [Episcopal] Church. At the council of 1868, which met at Lynchburg, Virginia, he had been sent as a delegate, and spent three days there. In 1869 "the council was to meet in Fredericksburg, Virginia, and he was again elected to represent his church."[331]

Toward the Sunset

Writing to his wife from Alexandria, Virginia, July 25, 1869, where he had gone to attend the funeral of his brother, Commodore Sydney Smith Lee, he closed,

May God bless you all and preserve us for the time when we too must part, the one from the other, which is now close at hand, and may we all meet again at the footstool of our merciful God, to be joined by His eternal love never more to separate.[332]

Godfather to Grandson

Sunday, August 1, 1869, while visiting his

A MAN OF PRAYER

son, Fitzhugh, at "White House," New Kent, Virginia, he attended service at Saint Peter's, the old Colonial church a few miles away, where George Washington and Mrs. Custis were married ninety years before. General Lee's grandson was christened, and he stood as godfather.

Desires to Visit Daughter's Grave

Being in poor health, his physicians and the college faculty urged him to go further south, to escape the rigors of a Lexington March. He made a six weeks' visit to Georgia and Florida, accompanied by his daughter Agnes. In fulfillment of a long-cherished desire, he planned to visit the grave of his daughter Annie, who had died during the war, in October, 1862, at Warren, White Sulphur Springs, North Carolina, at the age of twenty-three. At the close of the war, as has already been noted, the citizens of the country erected a fine monument over her grave. In a letter to his daughter Mildred, Monday, March 21, 1870, he said:

I wish also to visit my dear Annie's grave before I die. I have always desired to visit her grave since the cessation of active hostilities, but have never been able. I wish to see how calmly she sleeps away from us all, with her dear hands folded over her breast as if in mute prayer, while her pure spirit is traversing the land of the blessed.[333]

In a letter to his son, Fitzhugh, Tuesday, March 22, 1870, he said:

I shall go first to Warrenton Springs, North Carolina, to visit the grave of my dear Annie, where I have always promised myself to go, and I think, if I am to accomplish it, I have no time to lose. I wish to witness her quiet sleep, with her dear hands crossed over her breast, as it were in mute prayer, undisturbed by her distance from us, and to feel that her pure spirit is waiting in bliss in the land of the blessed.[334]

Visits Daughter's Grave

He visited his daughter's grave on Tuesday, April 2, 1870, and the same day wrote from Savannah, Georgia, to his wife at Lexington, saying,

My visit to dear Annie's grave was mournful, yet soothing to my feelings, and I was glad to have the opportunity of thanking the kind friends for their care of her while living and their attention to her since her death.[335]

Visits Mother's Girlhood Home

Returning from the South, he visited "Shirley," in Virginia, his mother's home when she was a girl, and where she was married to "Light Horse Harry." One of the daughters of the house, then a young girl, said:

"I can only remember the great dignity and

kindness of General Lee's bearing, how lovely he was to all of us girls, that he gave us his photographs and wrote his name on them. He liked to have us tickle his hands, but when Cousin Agnes [his daughter] came to sit by him, that seemed to be her privilege. We regarded him with the greatest veneration. We had heard of God, but here was General Lee!"[336]

CHAPTER XXIII

AN ACTIVE CHURCHMAN

ACTIVE IN CHURCH WORK

GENERAL LEE was a most active promoter of the interests of his church, and of the cause of Christ in the community; and all of the pastors felt that they had in him a warm friend.

He was a most liberal contributor to his church and to other objects of benevolence. At the vestry meeting over which he presided the evening he was taken with his fatal illness, an effort was being made to raise a certain sum for an important object. General Lee had already made an exceedingly liberal contribution, but when it was ascertained that $55 were still lacking, he quietly said, "I will give the balance." These were the last words he spoke in the meeting—his contribution, his last public act. Within the last twelve months of his life he gave $100 to the education of soldiers' orphans, $100 to the Young Men's Christian Association of the college and smaller sums to a number of similar objects—making, in the aggregate, a most liberal contribution.

His manner of giving was modest and un-

AN ACTIVE CHURCHMAN

ostentatious. In giving to Chaplain J. William Jones, the pastor, a very handsome contribution to the Lexington Baptist Church, he quietly said: "Will you do me the kindness to hand this to your treasurer, and save me the trouble of hunting him up? I am getting old now, and you young men must help me." His whole manner is described as that of one receiving instead of bestowing a favor.[337]

"Am I a Christian?"

Shortly before his death, when in the presence of a few friends who were warmly discussing a disputed doctrine of his church, his opinion was asked for. With great modesty and gentleness he answered, "I trouble myself but little about such things; my only concern is, am I really and truly a Christian?"[338]

At another time, he remarked to a friend, "It is my especial aim to feel that I am a Christian." The consecrated heart, the life hid with communion in God, was his test.[339]

A Word in Season

General Lee was not accustomed to talk of anything that concerned himself, and did not often speak freely of his inner religious feelings. Yet he would, when occasion offered, speak most decidedly of his reliance for salvation upon the merits of his personal Redeemer, and none who heard him thus talk could doubt for a moment that his faith was built on the "Rock of Ages."

He said to a friend in speaking of the duty of laboring for the good of others: "Ah! Mrs. P——, I find it so hard to keep one poor sinner's heart in the right way, that it seems presumptuous to try to help others."

And yet he did, quietly and unostentatiously, speak "a word in season" and exert influences potent for good in directing others in the path to heaven.[340]

Special Sins

One day he met a lady down in the town (Lexington), who bitterly complained that she could get nothing to eat in Lexington suitable for Lent—no fish, no oysters, etc.

The General replied,

I would not trouble myself so much about special dishes; I suppose if we try to abstain from special sins that is all that will be expected of us.[341]

Apostolic Succession

Someone asked him if he believed in the apostolic succession. He said he had never thought of it, and on another similar occasion, "I never trouble myself about such questions; my chief concern is to try to be a humble, sincere Christian myself."[342]

AN ACTIVE CHURCHMAN

Fasting During Lent

On one occasion someone asked Lee's opinion as to the practice of fasting during Lent and at other times. He spoke reverently of the church's requirements of its members, as to the practice, but added, "The best way for most of us is to fast from our sins and to eat what is good for us."[343]

His Great Mistake

He said to some of the professors in Washington College that, "The great mistake of my life was taking a military education."[344]

The Best Thing in the World

What General Lee thought was "the best thing in the world" is indicated by a remark made to Mr. Edward V. Valentine, the distinguished Virginia sculptor, of Richmond, in the summer of 1870, while he was making a bust of the General in Lexington.

"During the sittings," says Mr. Valentine, "I spoke of Major Stiles, of his cleverness, his culture, his bravery, and other attractive qualities, and the General added, 'and, better than all, he is a Christian gentleman.'"[345]

Summary of Christian Character

The religious phase of Lee's character may be summed up in three short sentences:

He trusted and loved God.

He loved his fellow men.

He believed in Jesus Christ as his Saviour and Lord, and manifested the Christian spirit toward enemies as well as friends.[346]

CHAPTER XXIV

GENERAL LEE AND THE BIBLE

Love for the Bible

The Bible was his daily companion, his guide, his comfort, and his trust. He was a constant reader, and a diligent student of God's Word, and had his regular seasons for this delightful exercise. In the army he read his Bible every day, in his headquarters, on the march, or in bivouac; and he did everything in his power to circulate the Word of God among his soldiers. The humble colporteur was always assured of a warm welcome at headquarters and an active helper in the Commander-in-Chief.[347]

Two Favorite Books

His two favorite books, which he always kept in his small private library, and which were in constant use, were the Episcopal *Prayer Book* and the Bible.[348]

His Favorite Hymn

"How firm a foundation, ye saints of the
 Lord,
Is laid for your faith in His excellent word!

What more can He say than to you He hath said,—
You who unto Jesus for refuge have fled?

. . . .

"The soul that on Jesus hath leaned for repose,
I will not, I will not desert to his foes;
That soul, though all hell should endeavor to shake,
I'll never, no never, no never, forsake!"

This was always a favorite hymn of General Lee's. At his burial, after the body was lowered into the vault, the congregation sang this hymn of assurance, which gave him courage "through the deep waters" and "through fiery trials."[349]

President of Bible Society

He always manifested the liveliest interest in giving to others the precious Bible. During the war he was an active promoter of Bible distribution among his soldiers, and soon after coming to Lexington he accepted the presidency of the Rockbridge Bible Society, and continued to discharge its duties up to the time of his death. Herewith is his letter accepting this office:

Gentlemen: I have delayed replying to your letter informing me of having been elected president of the "Rockbridge Bible Society," not for want of interest in the subject, but from an apprehension

GENERAL LEE AND THE BIBLE

that I should not be able to perform the duties of the position in such manner as to advance the high object proposed. Having, however, been encouraged by your kind assurances, and being desirous of co-operating, in any way I can, in extending the inestimable knowledge of the priceless truths of the Bible, I accept the position assigned me.

With many thanks to the society for the high compliment paid me by their selection as their president, I am, with great respect,

Your obedient servant,

R. E. LEE.

Rev. Dr. Pendleton,
Col. J. T. L. Preston, } *Committee.*[350]
Mr. Wm. White,

1868] [Age 61

TESTIMONIAL

The following action was taken by his associates after his death:

"At the meeting of the Board of Managers of the Rockbridge County Bible Society, on the 12th instant, for the purpose of imparting to the organization greater efficiency—in addition to other important measures adopted and in substance since published—the undersigned were appointed a committee to prepare and publish a minute, expressing the deep sense which the managers and members of this Society have of the exalted worth of their last president, the illustrious General R. E. Lee; of the blessed influence which he exerted as a Christian man and in his official relation to this cause, and of the grievous loss to us in removal, even to celestial joy.

"The duty is to us most grateful. World-wide and enduring as must be the renown of our honored friend for great abilities, grandeur of character and achievements, perhaps, in proportion to appliances, never surpassed—his crowning glory was, in our view, the sublime simplicity of his Christian faith and life. To the inviolable dignity of a soul among the noblest of all history was in him thoroughly united that guileless, unpretending, gentle and yet earnest spirit of a little child, so emphatically designated by our Lord as the essential characteristic of his chosen ones. These were the traits which, while they justly endeared him to children, and friends, and all the people, rendered him prompt to every, even the humblest duty, and caused him, although burdened with weighty cares, to accept the quietly useful task of presiding over so inconspicuous a good work as that of the Rockbridge County Bible Society. Of the judicious zeal with which he undertook this service, evidence conclusive was at once given in the wisely simple yet stirring appeal, which he penned and sent forth to the several ministers and congregations of the county, urging them to renewed energy in remedying Bible destitution throughout our borders. Well may the friends of this cause mourn the loss of such a leader, and record on the tablets of their hearts an example so good, as an incentive to their own efficiency for the future!

"In connection with this testimonial of the society's loving estimate of their last president, the undersigned were instructed to cause to be published the *Appeal* above referred to, written by General Lee's own hand, of which copies were at the time sent to all the ministers and congregations of the county. The original remains, a precious memento, in the archives of the society. To it, as hereunto subjoined in print, we ask the attentive consideration due alike to its great author and to the important cause for which he pleads. Facts and principles bearing on the question are to-day very much as they were five years ago, when the mind of this great and good man was moved so impressively to put them forth in the following circular.

"Although now resting from his labors, his works do follow him! Shall they not, in this and in other forms, effectually plead with all to be alive to Christian privilege in this matter, and faithful to duty therein and in all things?

"W. N. Pendleton,
"J. L. Clarke,   } *Committee*."³⁵¹
"J. W. Pratt,

The Appeal
(Written by General Lee's own hand)

Lexington, Va., January 14, 1869.

The Rockbridge County Bible Society, whose operations were interrupted and records lost during the war, was reorganized on the 5th of last October by representatives of different churches of the county, in pursuance of a notice given through the *Lexington Gazette*. A new constitution was adopted which provides for the reorganization of a Board of Managers, composed of the ministers of each church and one representative from each congregation, appointed by them, to meet at least once a year, on the first Saturday in October; and that the officers of the society shall be a President, a Vice-President, Secretary and Treasurer, and Librarian, who shall constitute the Executive Committee of the society.

At the meeting mentioned, the officers elected were:

R. E. Lee, President.

J. T. L. Preston, Vice-President.

Wm. G. White, Secretary and Treasurer.

John S. White, Librarian.

In compliance with a resolution of the meeting requesting the Executive Committee to take measures to procure a supply of Bibles, and to obtain from the congregations of the county funds for the purpose, it is respectfully requested that you will make, at the earliest and most suitable occasion, a collection in your congregation for this object, and cause the amount to be transmitted to the treasurer, Mr. Wm. G. White, at Lexington, and inform him at the same time, as far as practicable, how many copies of the Bible will be required to meet the wants of the congregation, as the constitution provides that each congregation shall mainly conduct the work of their distribution within their respective spheres.

The revival of the time-honored organization of the Rockbridge Bible Society, it is believed, will fill with pleasure the hearts of all good citizens in the county, and the Executive Committee earnestly appeal to the churches, their members, and all persons interested in the great work of the society, to unite cordially and promptly with them for its accomplishment. The first object is to supply every family with a copy of the Bible that is without it, and as many years have elapsed since there has been a distribution of the Holy Scriptures among us, it is feared, for reasons that are apparent, that there is at this time a great destitution among the people. The united and zealous efforts of all the denominations in the county are therefore earnestly solicited in aid of this good work.

Respectfully submitted,

R. E. LEE,
President Rockbridge Bible Society.[352]

Virginia Bible Society

General Lee was also deeply interested in the Virginia Bible Society and their noble work of giving the word of God to the people.

He wrote as follows to the president of that society:

Lexington, Virginia, April 5, 1869.

Rev. and Dear Sir: Your letter of first instant was only received this morning.

To reach Richmond by to-morrow evening, the anniversary of the Bible Society, I should have to ride all to-night to take the cars at Staunton to-morrow morning. I am suffering with a cold now, and fear the journey would lay me up.

I would, however, make the trial, did I think I could be of any service to the great object of the society. If the managers could suggest any plan, in addition to the abundant distribution of the Holy Scriptures, to cause the mass of the people to meditate on their simple truths, and, in the language of Wilberforce, "to read the Bible—read the Bible," so as to become acquainted with the experience and realities of religion, the greatest good would be accomplished. Wishing the society all success and continued advancement in its work,

I am, with great respect, most truly yours,

R. E. Lee.

Rev. Geo. Woodbridge, President Virginia Bible Society.[353]

CHAPTER XXV
THE SUNSET

His Last Public Act

The best account of General Lee's last days was written by Colonel William Preston Johnston, an intimate friend of the General and a distinguished member of the college Faculty. He was one of the watchers by his dying bedside. He was the son of General Albert Sidney Johnston, who fell at Shiloh.

"Wednesday, September 28, 1870, found General Lee at his post of duty. In the morning he was fully occupied with the correspondence and other tasks incident to his office of president of Washington College, and he declined offers of assistance from members of the Faculty, of whose services he sometimes availed himself. After dinner, at four o'clock, he attended a vestry meeting of Grace [Episcopal] Church [of which body he was a member. He was also a member of the building committee for the proposed new building]. The afternoon was chilly and wet, and a steady rain had set in, which did not cease until it resulted in a great flood, the most memorable and destructive in this region for a hundred years. The church was rather cold and damp, and General Lee, during the meeting, sat in a pew with his military cape cast loosely about him. In a conversation that occupied the brief space preceding the call to order, he took part, and told with marked cheerfulness of manner and kindliness of tone some pleasant anecdotes of Bishop Meade and Chief Justice Marshall.

"The meeting was protracted until after seven o'clock by a discussion touching the rebuilding of the church edifice and the increase of the rector's salary [the Rev. Dr. William N. Pendleton, formerly his chief of artillery]. General Lee acted as chairman, and, after hearing all that was said, gave his own opinion, as was his wont, briefly and without argument. He closed the meeting with a characteristic act. The amount required for the minister's salary lacked a sum much greater than General Lee's proportion of the subscription, in view of his frequent and generous contributions to the church and other charities, but just before the adjournment, when the treasurer announced the amount of the deficit still remaining [$55], General Lee said in a low tone, 'I will give that sum.' "[354]

The Appointed Hour Had Come

"General Lee returned to his house, and,

[1870   [Age 63

THE SUNSET

finding his family waiting tea for him, took his place at the table, standing to say grace. The effort was vain; the lips could not utter the prayer of the heart. Finding himself unable to speak, he took his seat quietly and without agitation. His face seemed to some of the anxious group about him to wear a look of sublime resignation, and to evince a full knowledge that the hour had come when all the cares and anxieties of his crowded life were at an end."[355]

He lingered nearly two weeks. In the words of his physician, "he neither expected nor desired to recover." When his son, General Custis Lee, made some allusion to his recovery, he shook his head and pointed upward.[356]

"He apparently knew from the first that the appointed hour had come when he must enter those dark gates that, closing, open no more to earth." "Soon after nine o'clock, on Wednesday morning, October 12, 1870, he closed his eyes, and his soul passed peacefully from earth."[357]

Last Words

His last words were, "Strike the tent." "Tell Hill he *must* come up," as if the great soldier felt he must move to a heavenly camping ground."[358]

An Irish orator said, "The solitude of George

Washington was broken as Lee crossed the threshold of heaven."[359]

His wife, in a letter to a dear friend, said, "And oh, what a glorious rest was in store for him!"[360]

"Passing Over the River"

The *Southern Collegian*, the organ of the students of Washington College, said,

"He died as he lived, calmly and quietly, in the full assurance of the Christian's faith, and with the brightest evidence that, in 'passing over the river,' he has (with his great lieutenant, 'Stonewall' Jackson) 'rested under the shade of the trees' of paradise."[361]

Victory Service

General Lee had won his greatest victory. "He lived the life of a faithful soldier of the cross—he fell at his post of duty—he died in the full assurance of faith in Jesus, and now wears the Christian's 'crown' which glittered to the eye of that Christian soldier who said, 'I have fought a good fight, I have finished my course, I have kept the faith; henceforth there is laid up for me a crown of righteousness, which the Lord, the righteous Judge, shall give me at that day.'"

"'But thanks be to God, which giveth us the victory through our Lord Jesus Christ.'"

"On Friday morning, October 14, 1870, the college chapel was filled at nine o'clock with a solemn congregation of students and citizens, all of whom seemed deeply moved by the simple exercises. The Rev. Dr. William N. Pendleton, his pastor, read from Psalm 37. 8-11 and 28-40, and with deep feeling applied its lessons to the audience, as illustrated in the life and death of General Lee. The speaker had for forty-five years been intimately associated with this great and good man as fellow student, comrade-in-arms, and pastor; and testified to his singular and consistent rectitude, dignity, and excellence under all the circumstances of life, and to that meekness in him that under the most trying adversity knew not envy, anger, or complaint. 'The law of God was in his heart,' therefore did 'none of his steps slide.' 'Mark the perfect man and behold the upright, for the end of that man is peace.' The minister powerfully illustrated the text of his discourse in the career of this great and good man, and urged his hearers to profit by the example of this servant of the Lord.

"The venerable Dr. W. S. White, 'Stonewall' Jackson's pastor, and the Rev. Dr. John William Jones, of the Baptist Church, who had served as chaplain in the Confederate Army, and had since been intimately connected with

General Lee, followed with brief but interesting remarks on the Christian character of the deceased."[362]

Burial

Saturday, October 15, 1870, was the day appointed for the burial. Colonel William Preston Johnston describes the service:

"The Rev. Dr. William N. Pendleton, rector of the Episcopal Church in Lexington, the long intimate personal friend of General Lee, his chief of artillery during the war, and his pastor the past five years, read the beautiful burial services of the Episcopal Church. No sermon was preached, and nothing said besides the simple service, in accordance with the known wishes of General Lee.

"After the funeral services were concluded in the chapel, the body was removed to the vault prepared for its reception, and the concluding services read by the chaplain from the bank on the southern side of the chapel, in front of the vault.

"There was sung, in the chapel, the 124th hymn of the Episcopal collection; and, after the coffin was lowered into the vault, the congregation sang the grand old hymn, 'How firm a foundation, ye saints of the Lord.' This was always a favorite hymn of General Lee's."[363]

Memorial Meetings

Saturday, October 15, 1870, the day of the funeral, was generally observed as a day of mourning throughout the South. Numerous memorial meetings were held. One was in the Masonic Temple, Baltimore. General William Preston, in his address, said:

"When I last saw him, the raven hair had turned white. In a small village church his reverent head was bowed in prayer. The humblest step was that of Robert E. Lee, as he entered the portals of the temple erected to God. In broken responses, he answered to the services of the church."[364]

Pocket Bible

Chaplain J. William Jones said, "As I watched alone by his body the day after his death, I picked up from the table a well-used pocket Bible, in which was written, in his characteristic chirography, 'R. E. Lee, Lieutenant-Colonel United States Army.' "[365]

"As I turned its leaves and saw how he had marked many passages, especially those teaching the great doctrines of salvation by grace, justification by faith, or those giving the more precious promises to the believer, I thought of how, with simple faith, he took this blessed book as the man of his counsel and the light of his pathway; how its precious promises cheered him amid the afflictions and trials of his eventful life; and how its glorious hope illumined for him 'the valley of the shadow of death.' "[366]

"He had God in his heart," which made him "a leader unlike the famous captains of the ages. Alexander believed in himself, Caesar in his legions, Napoleon in his destiny, Lee in his God."[367]

Test of a True Gentleman

Not long after General Lee's death, the Rev. J. William Jones found the following memorandum in his own handwriting, among some loose sheets in his army satchel, which had not been disturbed since his return from Appomattox Court House:

The forbearing use of power does not only form a touchstone, but the manner in which an individual enjoys certain advantages over others is a test of a *true gentleman*. The power which the strong have over the weak, the magistrate over the citizen, the employer over the employed, the educated over the unlettered, the experienced over the confiding, even the clever over the silly—the forbearing or inoffensive use of all this power or authority, or a total abstinence from it when the case admits it, will show the gentleman in a plain light. The gentleman does not needlessly remind an offender of a wrong he may have committed against him. He cannot only forgive, he can forget; and he strives for that nobleness of self and mildness of character which impart sufficient strength to let the past be but the past. *A true man of honor feels humbled himself when he cannot help humbling others.*[368]

A Christian Gentleman

General Lee was the noblest type of the Christian gentleman, as those who knew him bear witness:

"The most manly and entire gentleman I ever saw," was the way Alexander H. Stephens spoke of him.[369]

"The most chivalrous gentleman in the world," wrote John H. Mitchell, the Irish patriot.[370]

"Among men noble as the noblest, in the lofty dignity of the Christian gentleman."[371]

"Lee was, and is, my beau-ideal of the highest type of Christian gentleman," said Rev. Edward Clifford Gordon, who was officially connected with Washington College when Lee was president.[372]

CHAPTER XXVI

TESTIMONY OF ASSOCIATES

Lee's Soldiers

The day after his death a meeting of the officers and soldiers of the Confederate Army resident in Rockbridge assembled in Lexington, Virginia, and unanimously adopted the following resolution:

"1. *Resolved*, That, as humble members of the great army of which General Robert Edward Lee was the illustrious head and chief, we mourn his death. With feelings untinged by bitter memories of a stormy past, and with no vain thought of exalting his name in the opinion of mankind, we meet to do him honor. At his open grave passion must stand abashed, and eulogy is dumb. Striving to mount up to that clear air, wherein his own spirit dwelt, of calm wisdom and heroic patience, we seek only to render a last, simple, but just tribute to his memory. At different times he was known to some or all of us from the day that he received the sword of Virginia at the hands of her sovereign convention, and from the seven days around Richmond, through the varying fortunes of an unequal fight, to the closing scenes at Appomattox. He has been known to us again as the beloved and venerated citizen of our own community, and the president of the noble institution of learning to which George Washington gave an endowment and a name. We have been daily witness to his quiet, unostentatious, Christian life; we have seen him prove that 'him no adversity could ever move, nor policy at any time entice to shrink from God and from His word.' Knowing him, as we thus did, in war and in peace, we pronounce him to have been, in all the elements of real greatness which may challenge cavil and defy the touch of time, the peer of the most renowned of any age or country and the foremost American of the wondrous century in which he lived.

"He is gone from among us—'gone before the Father; far beyond the twilight judgments of this world; high above its mists and obscurities'—no more shall we look upon his noble form, meet his benignant smile, or receive his kindly greeting. But here, where he set his last great example of steadfast, unselfish devotion to duty, the memory of his greatness and his worth must ever linger; and, while we reverently bow in submission to the summons of Infinite Wisdom calling him away, we send up a solemn aspiration of thankfulness that to us was the honor and the blessing of communion with him in his last days on earth, and to our people is committed the pious office of consigning his mortal remains to the tomb. Hallowed, through all time, shall be the spot whence his spirit passed from earth to heaven!"[373]

Washington College Faculty

The Faculty of Washington College took appropriate action, saying, "As president, in his relations to the Faculty, he was gentle, courteous, and considerate—toward the students he was firm in discipline, yet forbearing, sympathetic, and encouraging—to all he was a model of an elevated Christian and an upright gentleman."[374]

Colonel William Preston Johnston

At a meeting of the Faculty and students of Washington College, Colonel William Preston Johnston, professor of history and literature, said:

"In all the recorded past, no epoch has excelled in luster and development the period of Pericles, when free Athens under his enlightened guidance made herself immortal. The republic whose citizens are gathered this morning within these walls has obeyed with willing hearts a leader who had the virtues of Pericles, without one blemish, one spot, one stain. In him duty disdained to yield to expediency, and Aristides himself would have owned him as a peer in virtue. It was the dying boast of Pericles that he had made no Athenian weep; but of our chief it may be said that for no act of his has any son of the South ever had cause to blush. With such a leader, with such an examplar before our eyes, it has not been hard to do right. It would have been hard to do wrong, to go far astray, and face our consciences in that august presence."[375]

Fitzhugh Lee

His nephew, Fitzhugh Lee, cavalry commander, son of Commodore Sydney Smith Lee, speaks of him as "a perfect and beautiful model of manhood." "The profession of the soldier has been honored by his renown, the cause of education by his virtue, religion by his piety."[376]

Robert E. Lee, Jr.

His son, Robert Edward, said, "His was a practical, everyday religion, which supported him all through his life, enabled him to bear with equanimity every reverse of fortune, and to accept her gifts without undue elation."[377]

Jefferson Davis

In an address at a gathering of Lee's veterans

at Richmond, Virginia, Thursday, November 3, 1870, Jefferson Davis paid the following tribute to General Lee: "This good citizen, this gallant soldier, this great general, this true patriot, had yet a higher praise than this, or these—*he was a true Christian*. The Christianity that ennobled his life gives us the consolatory belief that he is happy beyond the grave."[378]

Alexander H. Stephens

Alexander H. Stephens, Vice-President of the Confederate States, said, "What I had seen of General Lee to be at first—childlike in simplicity and unselfish in his character—he remained, unspoiled by praise and success."[379]

Rev. Dr. J. William Jones

Chaplain J. William Jones, and pastor of the Baptist Church in Lexington, Virginia, while Lee was president of Washington College, speaks from an intimate personal acquaintance and knowledge:

"If I have ever come in contact with a sincere, devout Christian, one who, seeing himself to be a sinner, trusted alone in the merits of Christ—who humbly tried to walk the path of duty, 'looking unto Jesus' as the author and finisher of his faith—and whose piety constantly exhibited itself in his daily life—that man was General R. E. Lee."[380]

Rev. Dr. W. T. Brantly

From a sermon at the Second Baptist Church, Atlanta, Georgia, by the pastor, the Rev. Dr. W. T. Brantly, on the death of Lee:

"It was my privilege, the past two years, to be thrown into his society, at different times, so intimately that I saw and conversed with him every day and frequently several times a day. I discovered that, with him, religion was a theme on which he most delighted to dwell. He spoke to me with great interest of the efforts made by different denominations of Christian people to promote the spiritual good of the soldiers. He took pleasure in referring to the numbers who, he hoped, had been brought to the Saviour through the instrumentality of the chaplains and visiting ministers.

"Speaking to me, last June, of the college under his control, he referred more than once, evidently with the greatest satisfaction, to the number of students who had been hopefully converted during the term then just closed. He also mentioned with much interest the work of the Young Men's Christian Association among the students."[381]

Rev. Dr. T. V. Moore

In a memorial address, Saturday, October 15, 1870, the day of Lee's funeral, in the First

Presbyterian Church, Nashville, Tennessee, the Rev. Dr. T. V. Moore, the pastor, summed up General Lee's "unselfish nobleness," as follows:

"Other men have been great warriors, yet only great in success. It was his to show his uttermost greatness in failure. Other men had conquered victory; it was his sublime pre-eminence to conquer defeat, and transform it into the grandest triumph. Other warriors have betrayed ambition, cruelty, and avarice in success, weakness, littleness, and selfishness in disaster; but he developed the unselfish nobleness of his nature when, bowing submissively to the resistless decrees of Providence, he sheathed his unsullied blade; and refusing the most tempting offers to engage in commercial and monetary enterprises; refusing the gifts that a grateful though impoverished people longed to lavish on him; refusing every attempt to bring him where public applause would so heartily have greeted him—he retired to the cloistered shades of his chosen position, without a word of repining, and consecrated himself to the youth of his country, not to breathe into them a spirit of vindictive hate; not to train them for future political struggles only, but to lead them to Jesus, and make them noble citizens, by making them sincere Christians."[382]

TESTIMONY OF ASSOCIATES

Professor Edward S. Joynes

Professor Edward S. Joynes, a member of the Faculty of Washington College under General Lee, in an address at the University of South Carolina, January 19, 1907, said:

"Of General Lee's religious character I do not feel myself worthy to speak.

"That he was deeply, sincerely religious, with a perfect, trusting faith in God and in Christ—that by this he was guided and upborne in every act and every trial—that this he sought unobtrusively yet earnestly to impress upon his family, his community, his college, as he had done upon the army—this is manifest from all the course of his life, as from his writings. His last afternoon was spent in a vestry meeting —at which I also was present—in the attempt to relieve his beloved rector (formerly his trusted companion in arms), and his last conscious act was, on that same evening, to attempt to ask a blessing upon the evening meal—when God called him, and he sank in his chair. Of the following days of anxious sorrow, of the shock of his death, and of the grief with which we laid him in his coffin and followed him to his grave, I have no heart to speak.

"There he rests beneath the chapel which he himself built to the glory of God—his tomb fitly crowned with that recumbent statue by Valentine, symbol of the Eternal Rest."[383]

"A Royal Soul Within a Royal Body"

Lee's personal appearance was very striking. A mental picture will help to understand his character. As a young man, the description by his friends and associates is very interesting:

"As fine-looking a man as one would wish to see, a perfect figure and strikingly handsome," is the description by General Henry J. Hunt.[384]

"A man then in the vigor of youthful strength, with a noble and commanding presence, and an admirable, graceful, and athletic figure," said General Montgomery C. Meigs.[385]

"He had a finished form, delicate hands; was graceful in person," said General John S. Preston.[386]

"My father never could bear to have his picture taken and there are no likenesses of him that really give his sweet expression," said his son, Captain Robert E. Lee.[387]

"Possessed of extraordinary manly beauty, both of face and form, he had a strength of body, and a capacity for action, for endurance of hunger, fatigue, and exposure, which has rarely ever been equaled," said General Lawton.[388]

Other observers add to the charming impression of his kingly stature:

"The admirable symmetry of his person and the manly beauty of his countenance were the aids to his virtue which secured to him tolerance, affection, and respect from all with whom he mingled."[389]

"General Lee was a notably handsome man. He was tall of stature [5 feet, 11 inches], and admirably proportioned; his features were regular and most amiable in appearance, and in his manners he was courteous and dignified."[390]

"With a chivalric soul beaming from every feature."

"A countenance which beamed with gentleness and benevolence."[391]

"A bearing, simple, graceful, and natural, in which there was modesty without diffidence, and supreme dignity without assertion."[392]

"His splendid physique, grand carriage without 'airs,' universal politeness, and evident kind heart, impressed me greatly."[393]

"No representation of General Lee which I have ever seen properly conveys the light and softness of his eye, the tenderness and intellectuality of his mouth, or the indescribable refinement of his face. Robert E. Lee was incomparably the greatest-looking man I ever saw."[394]

"The most striking figure we have ever encountered, erect as a poplar, yet lithe and graceful, with broad shoulders well thrown back, a finely, justly proportioned head posed in unconscious dignity, clear, deep, thoughtful eyes, and the quiet, dauntless step of one every inch the gentleman and soldier."[395]

"Stonewall" Jackson said, "General Lee is the most perfect animal form I ever saw."

CHAPTER XXVII

TRIBUTES

London Standard

The London *Standard* said:

"Truer greatness, a loftier nature, a spirit more merciful, a character purer, more chivalrous, the world has rarely, if ever, known.

"Of stainless hue and deep religious feeling, yet free from all taint and cant and fanaticism, and as dear and congenial to the cavalier Stuart as to the puritan "Stonewall" Jackson; unambitious, but ready to sacrifice all to the call of duty; devoted to his cause, yet never moved by his feelings beyond the line prescribed by his judgment; never provoked by just resentment to punish wanton cruelty by reprisals which would have given a character of needless savagery to the war; both North and South owe a debt of gratitude to him, and the time will come when both will be equally proud of him.

"A country which has given birth to men like him, may look the chivalry of Europe in the face without shame; for the *fatherlands of Sidney and Bayard never produced a nobler soldier, gentleman, and Christian than General Robert Edward Lee.*"[396]

New York Herald

The New York *Herald* said:

"As a slaveholder he was beloved by his slaves for his kindness and consideration toward them. General Lee was also noted for his piety. He was an Episcopalian, and was a regular attendant at church. Having a perfect command of his temper, he was never seen angry, and his most intimate friends never heard him utter an oath. Indeed, it is doubtful if there are many men of the present generation who unite so many virtues and so few vices in each of themselves as did General Lee. He came nearer the ideal of a soldier and Christian general than any man we can think of, for he was a greater soldier than Havelock, and equally as devout a Christian."[397]

New York Sun

The New York *Sun*, edited by Charles A. Dana, Mr. Lincoln's Assistant Secretary of War, thus concludes its notice of Lee's death:

"Whatever may be the verdict as to his career in public life, the universal expression will be that in General Lee an able soldier, a sincere Christian, and an honest man, has been taken from earth."[398]

Blackwood's Magazine

An English soldier, Colonel Lawler, who visited Lee at his headquarters during the war, wrote in *Blackwood's Magazine:*

"When the passions of the great Civil War shall have died out, Lee will be regarded more as a man than as a soldier. His infinite purity, self-denial, tenderness, and generosity, will make his memory more and more precious to his countrymen when they have purged their minds of the prejudices and animosities which civil war invariably breeds. They will acknowledge before long that Lee took no step in life except in accordance with what he regarded as, and believed to be, his duty."[399]

Confederate Veteran

Mr. John B. Collyar, a student at Washington College when Lee was president, in the *Confederate Veteran*, said:

"I dare say no man ever offered to relate a story of questionable delicacy in his presence. His very bearing and presence produced an atmosphere of purity that would have repelled the attempt."[400]

Southern Historian

A southern historian says:

"One may search in vain for any defect in

him. Indeed, the perfection of Lee becomes somewhat oppressive. One would welcome the discovery of a shortcoming in him, as redeeming him to humanity."[401]

Viscount Wolseley

The great British general, Viscount Wolseley, visited General Lee in the army in 1862. After Lee's death, he wrote:

"I desire to make known to the reader not only the renowned soldier, whom I believe to have been the greatest of his age, but to give some insight into the character of one whom I have always considered the most perfect man I ever met."[402]

Senator Benjamin Hill

In a memorial address, Senator Benjamin Hill, of Georgia, in beautiful phrase declaimed:

"He was a foe without hate, a friend without treachery, a soldier without cruelty, and a victim without murmuring. He was a public officer without vices, a private citizen without wrong, a neighbor without reproach, a Christian without hypocrisy, and a man without guile. He was Cæsar without his ambition, Frederick without his tyranny, Napoleon without his selfishness, and Washington without his reward. He was as obedient to authority as a servant and royal in authority as a king. He was as gentle as a woman in life, pure and modest as a virgin in thought, watchful as a Roman vestal, submissive to law as Socrates, and grand in battle as Achilles."[403]

CHAPTER XXVIII

HIS CROWNING GRACE

GOD IN HIS HEART

"EVERYWHERE and always, he had God in his heart, not so much the God of power, or the God of justice, or even the God of beauty, but the God of love, tempering the austerity of virtue, sweetening the bitterness of failure, above all, breathing loving-kindness into the intolerable hell of war. There have been fierce saints who were fighters. There have been gentle saints who were martyrs. It is rare to find a soldier making war—stern war—with the pity, the tenderness, the sympathy of a true follower of Christ."[404]

"Can there be any other inference save that Christianity supplied the unseen but mighty power which lifted Lee in the sphere of moral greatness so far above most of the great captains of history; that he drew the inspiration for these his greatest achievements from Heaven, not from earth; that it was divine grace and not nature that made his life so sublime?"[405]

"The crowning grace of this man, who was thus not only great but good, was the humility and trust in God which lay at the foundation of his character."[406]

"This meek and lowly trust in Jesus Christ and Him crucified is the key to his character."[407]

"His crowning glory was the sublime simplicity of His Christian faith and life."[408]

Sublime Heights

"It would be difficult to find, if not unreasonable to seek, a man of Lee's character and mind in the world of to-day; his mind dominated by his character; his character subject to the ruling force of veneration for his God. Lee's devotion is not to be readily comprehended by our modern world. We must look deeper, go farther horizons, than most men look to-day. Lee gave himself to God, living in a kind of spiritual harmony with Deity; closer to his conception of Deity than to any living being. By prayer he came into the presence of his God until he could see and feel Deity like an animate thing. . . .

"Long hours upon bended knees, on the fringes of the wilderness, at the dawns of conflicts, gave him spiritual strength verging upon the exalted. It was then he stepped from his tent twice-armed, black Perry (his servant) standing by a little awed, his staff waiting, bearing upon his face the calm that comes to

252 ROBERT E. LEE THE CHRISTIAN

devoted men from their God alone. Calm and
resolution; certitude of purpose; without doubt
in any degree, fighting the Lord's battle. The
Lord would sustain him. If not (did Lee ever
reason so far?), the Lord's will be done. Even
in defeat he had the humility to see Deity's
will for final good. No matter what might
eventuate, he would do his part, leave the rest
to God. . . .

"Where find such a man in this day? To
comprehend Lee in the least—vision him as a
man given to God, without question, without
demand, surrendered unto Deity as men did in
the early ages of Christianity. From devotion
to adoration had been an easy advance for Lee.
To him God was in everything, always present,
forever active, omniscient, the only and ever
perfect."[409]

"Every action of his life led to the satisfaction of his inner urging toward morality
and honor. It may be doubted whether Lee
ever committed an act that would reflect upon
his moral self, weighed in the court of his
consciousness. Or, having committed it, he
would be the man to erase the stain by prayer
and contrition. His purity of thought and
deed amounted to the virginal."[410]

"General Lee was a man who strengthened
the faith of mankind in the religion of Jesus

HIS CROWNING GRACE

Christ by the sublime heights to which Divine Grace so easily bore him."[411]

Majestic Personality

"His virtues, like his religion, were of large, simple, antique mold. His soul, mellowed, chastened, ennobled by suffering, gravely yet nobly borne, had, as it were, 'a look southward, and was open to the beneficent noon of Nature,' and Deity.

"He could no more have stooped to a meanness than he could voluntarily have committed moral suicide! A broad, unsophisticated, child-like, medieval nature was his, infinitely uplifted, gloriously enlightened by a modern culture, and all the graces and amenities of a true Christian discipleship. Take him all in all, he stands, morally, alone.

"Conventional standards of comparison fail us here. We cast aside our petty rules, our ordinary methods of inference, our poor standard measurements of everyday character, our common judgments, too small by far to embrace a majestic personality like this."[412]

Abraham Lincoln's Tribute to General Lee

On the morning of the day on which President Lincoln was assassinated, Friday, April 14,

1865, his son, Captain Robert Lincoln, came into the room with a photograph of General Lee in hand, which he had brought from Appomattox, where he had witnessed the surrender of Lee the Sunday before. The President, at breakfast, took the picture, laid it on the table before him, scanned the face thoughtfully, and said: "It is a good face; it is the face of a noble, noble, brave man. I am glad that the war is over."[413]

The Ideal Man

"In his civil, social, and domestic relations—as the citizen, companion, friend, husband, father, the wise instructor of the young, and, in one comprehensive phrase, as the Christian gentleman—

"In all such relations he appears to have been perfect. We scarcely exaggerate in saying that, since the death of the last of the evangelists [the Apostle John], probably no mortal man has passed through life, 'walking habitually nearer to his God,' in thought, conversation, worship, sublime simplicity of faith, in action, whose watchword was duty; and devout contemplation, soothed by the spirit and promises of the redeeming Christ!"[414]

"THE CARDINAL FACT OF LEE'S LIFE WAS GOD."
"LEE HAD ONE INTIMATE FRIEND—GOD."[415]

SOURCES OF INFORMATION

Following is a list of sixty books, magazines, and papers from which quotations have been made. Many of these books are out of print but may be found in libraries. The first word is the key-word used in references under "Where Found," page 261.

Adams: *John Quincy Adams, Writings*, 7 Vols., Vol. VII, p. 298.

Alexander: *Military Memoirs of a Confederate*, by General E. P. Alexander.

Bar: *Washington, Lee, and Lincoln*, American Bar Association. Dallas, Texas, 1924.

Blackwood: *Blackwood's Magazine*, London, England, 1870.

Bradford: *Lee the American*, by Gamaliel Bradford. Houghton Mifflin Company, Boston and New York, 1912. Quotations by special permission.

Brock: *Robert Edward Lee, Soldier, Citizen and Christian Patriot*, by Brock. 1897.

Bruce: *Robert E. Lee*, by Philip Alexander Bruce, 1907. W. B. Jacobs & Company, Philadelphia, Pa.

Camp: *Christ in the Camp*, by Rev. J. William Jones, D.D. B. F. Johnson & Co., Richmond, Virginia, 1897.

Doctor Jones was in the army of General Lee as a private soldier or chaplain, from Harpers Ferry in 1861 to Appomattox Court House in

1865. After the war he was pastor of the Baptist Church in Lexington, Virginia, and enjoyed in an unusual degree his favor and regard. During this period, and while acting at times as chaplain of Washington College, he had special opportunities to observe the character of General Lee.

Chautauquan: *The Chautauquan*, Vol. XXXI, 1900—"The Inner Life of Lee," by Chaplain Jones.

Chesney: *Military Biography*, by Colonel Charles Cornwallis Chesney. London, England.

Childe: *Life and Campaigns of General Lee*, by E. L. Childe (translated from French).

Clarke: *Colonial Churches*, by W. M. Clarke. 1907.

Collegian: *The Southern Collegian*, the organ of the students of Washington College, 1870.

Confederate: *The Confederate Cause and Conduct of the War.*

Cooke: *A Life of General Robert E. Lee*, by John Esten Cooke. D. Appleton & Co., New York, 1871.

Dabney: *Life and Campaigns of General T. J. Jackson*, 1864-66, by R. L. Dabney. Two volumes.

Diary: *A Rebel War Clerk's Diary*, by J. B. Jones.

Faculty: Records of the Meetings of the Faculty of Washington College, Commencing February 24, 1857.

Hayne: Paul H. Hayne—in Jones (2).

Herald: New York *Herald*, 1870.

Holcombe: Memorial Address by James P. Holcombe, LL.D., at Washington and Lee University, January 19, 1871.

SOURCES OF INFORMATION

Hosmer: *The Appeal to Arms*, by J. K. Hosmer. Harper & Brothers, New York, 1907. Quotations by special permission.

Johnstone (1): *Abraham Lincoln the Christian*, by William J. Johnstone. The Abingdon Press, New York, 1913.

Johnstone (2): *George Washington the Christian*, by William J. Johnstone. The Abingdon Press, New York, 1913.

Jones (1): *Life and Letters of General Robert E. Lee*, by J. William Jones. The Neale Publishing Co., New York. Quotations by special permission.

Jones (2): *Personal Reminiscences, Anecdotes, and Letters of General Robert E. Lee*, by Rev. J. William Jones, D.D. D. Appleton & Co., New York, 1875.

Joynes: "Lee the College President," Address by Prof. Edward S. Joynes, at University of South Carolina, January 19, 1907.

Keckley: *Behind the Scenes*, by Elizabeth Keckley. G. W. Carleton & Co., New York, 1868.

Keyes: *Fifty Years' Observation of Men and Events*, by Ed. Keyes.

Lee (1): *General Lee*, by Fitzhugh Lee, His Nephew. D. Appleton & Co., New York, 1895. Quotations by special permission.

Lee (2): *Recollections and Letters of General Robert E. Lee*, by his Son, Captain Robert E. Lee. Doubleday, Page & Co., New York, 1904. Quotations by special permission.

Legion: *American Legion Weekly*.

Leslie: "Recollections of My Father," by Captain Robert E. Lee, in *Frank Leslie's Monthly*, 1906.

Letter: Letter presented to the Virginia Historical Society, Richmond, Virginia, by Miss Mary Cushing Dame, granddaughter of the Rev. Cornelius Walker, in 1932.

Lippincott: Article by Mrs. Pickett in *Lippincott's Magazine*. Vol. 79.

Long: *Memoirs of General Robert E. Lee*, by General A. L. Long. J. M. Stoddard & Co., New York, 1887.

Mason: *Popular Life of General Robert E. Lee*, by Emily V. Mason. J. Murphy & Co., Baltimore, Maryland, 1874.

McKim: *The Soul of Lee*, by Randolph H. McKim. Longmans, Green & Co., New York, 1918. Quotations by special permission.

Moore: Memorial Discourse, First Presbyterian Church, Nashville, Tennessee, by the Rev. Dr. T. V. Moore, Sunday, October 25, 1870. Doctor Moore was pastor of the First Presbyterian Church, Richmond, Virginia, for many years, and afterward pastor of the First Presbyterian Church, Nashville, Tennessee.

Notebook: The Author's, often without notation of source.

Outlook: *The Outlook*, Vol. LVI.

Page (1): *Robert E. Lee, Man and Soldier*, by Thomas Nelson Page. Charles Scribner's Sons, New York, 1911. Quotations by special permission.

SOURCES OF INFORMATION 259

Page (2): *Robert E. Lee, the Southerner*, by Thomas Nelson Page. Charles Scribner's Sons, 1908. Quotations by special permission.

Pendleton (1): "Lee, the American," by Rev. Dr. and Gen. William N. Pendleton, in *Southern Magazine*, Vol. XV.

Pendleton (2): *Memoirs of William Nelson Pendleton, D.D.*, by Susan P. Lee.

Records (1): *Official Records of the Union and Confederate Armies*, Vol. XXIX.

Records (2): *Official Records of the Union and Confederate Armies*, Vol. LX.

Riley: *General Robert E. Lee After Appomattox*, by Franklin L. Riley, Professor of History in Washington and Lee University. The Macmillan Company, 1922. Quotations by special permission.

Shepherd: *Life of Robert Edward Lee*, by Henry F. Shepherd, M.A., LL.D. Neale Publishing Co., New York, 1906.

Smith: *Robert E. Lee, A Character Sketch*, by H. H. Smith, Ashland, Virginia.

Standard: The London *Standard*, 1870.

Stiles: *Four Years With Marse Robert*, by Robert Stiles. Neale Publishing Co., New York, 1904.

Sun: The New York *Sun*, 1870.

Telegraph: Montreal *Telegraph*, Montreal, Canada, 1870.

Veteran: *The Confederate Veteran*, Vol. I, 1893.

Whipple: *The Heart of Lee*, by Wayne Whipple. G. W. Jacobs & Co., Philadelphia, 1918.

White: *Robert E. Lee and the Southern Confederacy*,

by Henry Alexander White, Professor of History in Washington and Lee University. G. P. Putnam's Sons, New York, 1911. Quotations by special permission.

Wise: *The End of an Era*, by J. S. Wise.

Wolseley: *General Lee*, by Viscount Wolseley. George P. Humphrey, Rochester, New York, 1906.

Young: *Marse Robert, Knight of the Confederacy*, by James C. Young. Rae D. Henkle, Inc., New York, 1929.

WHERE FOUND

The numbers correspond to the index numbers throughout the book.

The name is the key-word used under "Sources of Information," page 255.

[1] Long, p. 34.
[2] McKim, p. 205.
[3] Chesney—in Jones (2), p. 72.
[4] Jones (2), p. 359.
[5] Jones (2), p. 360.
[6] Jones (2), p. 360.
[7] Mason, p. 9.
[8] Holcombe—in Jones (2), p. 489.
[9] White, p. 17.
[10] White, p. 17.
[11] White, p. 24.
[12] Young, p. 22.
[13] Mason, p. 18.
[14] Jones (2), p. 436.
[15] White, p. 24.
[16] Lee (1), p. 21.
[17] White, p. 17.
[18] Holcombe—in Jones (2), p. 489.
[19] Mason, p. 22.
[20] Wolseley, p. 13.
[21] Mason, p. 21.
[22] Clarke, p. 138.

[23] Jones (2), p. 362.
[24] Lee (1), p. 21.
[25] Jones (2), p. 489.
[26] Mason, p. 26.
[27] Page (2), p. 10.
[28] Long, p. 31.
[29] White, p. 26.
[30] Jones (2), p. 365.
[31] Long, p. 27.
[32] Long, p. 26.
[33] Long, p. 291.
[34] McKim, p. 203.
[35] Long, p. 29.
[36] Bradford, p. 8.
[37] Lee (2), p. 326.
[38] Long, p. 35.
[39] Long, p. 44.
[40] Jones (2), p. 373.
[41] Jones (2), p. 369.
[42] Long, p. 66.
[43] Jones (2), p. 370.
[44] Jones (2), p. 371.
[45] Jones (1), p. 52.
[46] Long, p. 62.
[47] Lee (2), p. 6.
[48] Lee (2), p. 6.
[49] Lee (2), p. 6.
[50] Jones (1), p. 72.
[51] Jones (1), p. 77.
[52] Bar, p. 19.
[53] Leslie—in Jones (1), p. 65.

WHERE FOUND

[54] Lee (2), p. 19.
[55] Holcombe—in Jones (2), p. 491.
[56] Long, p. 484.
[57] Holcombe—in Jones (2), p. 493.
[58] Pendleton, p. 605.
[59] Clarke, p. 138.
[60] Lee (1), p. 60.
[61] Lee (1), p. 61.
[62] Whipple, p. 87.
[63] Whipple, p. 88.
[64] Jones (1), p. 84.
[65] Lee (1), p. 68.
[66] Lee (1), p. 68.
[67] Lee (1), p. 69.
[68] Jones (1), p. 84.
[69] Lippincott, p. 52.
[70] Smith, p. 21.
[71] Jones (2), p. 382.
[72] Jones (1), p. 93.
[73] Jones (1), p. 99.
[74] Jones (1), p. 99.
[75] Jones (1), p. 119.
[76] Lee (2), p. 23.
[77] Lee (1), p. 84.
[78] Jones (1), p. 122.
[79] Bradford, p. 28.
[80] Bradford, p. 44.
[81] McKim, p. 26.
[82] Johnstone (2), p. 67.
[83] Johnstone (1), p. 74.
[84] Lee (2), p. 24.

[85] Lee (2), p. 25.
[86] Lee (2), p. 26.
[87] Clarke, p. 138.
[88] Lee (2), p. 28.
[89] Lee (2), p. 27.
[90] Jones (2), p. 138.
[91] Page (2), p. 54.
[92] Lee (1), p. 79.
[93] Jones (1), p. 135.
[94] Long, p. 102.
[95] Lee (2), p. 29.
[96] Lee (2), p. 29.
[97] Lee (2), p. 30.
[98] Lee (2), p. 30.
[99] Lee (2), p. 30.
[100] Lee (2), p. 30.
[101] Letter.
[102] Johnstone (1), p. 69.
[103] Lee (1), p. 94.
[104] Jones (1), p. 141.
[105] Lee (2), p. 32.
[106] Lee (2), p. 35.
[107] Lee (1), p. 98.
[108] Bradford, p. 92.
[109] Records (1), p. 722.
[110] Jones (2), p. 409.
[111] Lee (2), p. 37.
[112] Lee (2), p. 39.
[113] Lee (2), p. 41.
[114] Lee (2), p. 42.
[115] Camp, p. 79.

WHERE FOUND

[116] Camp, p. 79.
[117] Jones (1), p. 147.
[118] Lee (2), p. 44.
[119] Lee (2), p. 45.
[120] Jones (1), p. 148.
[121] Lee (2), p. 49.
[122] Lee (2), p. 50.
[123] Lee (2), p. 55.
[124] Lee (2), p. 55.
[125] Lee (2), p. 56.
[126] Lee (2), p. 58.
[127] Lee (2), p. 58.
[128] Jones (1), p. 156.
[129] Long, p. 23.
[130] Lee (2), p. 63.
[131] Lee (2), p. 64.
[132] Jones (2), p. 388.
[133] Lee (2), p. 66.
[134] Lee (2), p. 67.
[135] Camp, p. 69.
[136] Lee (2), p. 68.
[137] Long, p. 168.
[138] Mason, p. 110.
[139] Lee (2), p. 70.
[140] Lee (2), p. 70.
[141] Lee (2), p. 74.
[142] Mason, p. 117.
[143] Lee (2), p. 75.
[144] Camp, p. 49.
[145] Jones (2), p. 392.
[146] Mason, p. 375.

[147] Lee (2), p. 79.
[148] Lee (2), p. 80.
[149] Lee (2), p. 81.
[150] Jones (1), p 262.
[151] Jones (2), p. 155.
[152] Lee (2), p. 87.
[153] Lee (2), p. 88.
[154] Camp, p. 55.
[155] Page (2), p. 31.
[156] Lee (1), p. 71.
[157] Lee (2), p. 90.
[158] Lee (1), p. 84.
[159] Confederate, p. 22.
[160] Lee (2), p. 93.
[161] Camp, p. 55.
[162] Camp, p. 488.
[163] Jones (2), p. 152.
[164] Jones (2), p. 152.
[165] Camp, p. 55.
[166] Mason, p. 182.
[167] Jones (2), p. 153.
[168] Jones (2), p. 153.
[169] Moore, p. 10.
[170] Shepherd, p. 52.
[171] Camp, p. 51.
[172] Jones (2), p. 73.
[173] Jones (2), p. 319.
[174] Lee (2), p. 95.
[175] Lee (2), p. 96.
[176] Lee (2), p. 97.
[177] Jones (2), p. 187.

WHERE FOUND

[178] Long, p. 272.
[179] Mason, p. 211.
[180] Bruce, p. 359.
[181] Lee (2), p. 101.
[182] Lee (2), p. 108.
[183] Jones (1), p. 288.
[184] Jones (2), p. 400.
[185] Lee (2), p. 101.
[186] Lee (2), p. 105.
[187] Camp, p. 56.
[188] Bradford, p. 117.
[189] Bradford, p. 242.
[190] Bradford, p. 240.
[191] Lee (2), p. 110.
[192] Lee (2), p. 111.
[193] Lee (2), p. 113.
[194] Lee (2), p. 116.
[195] Jones (2), p. 173.
[196] Lee (2), p. 117.
[197] Camp, p. 50.
[198] Records (2), p. 1150.
[199] Camp, p. 59.
[200] Long, p. 350.
[201] Jones (2), p. 184.
[202] Jones (2), p. 401.
[203] Jones (2), p. 168.
[204] Bradford, p. 121.
[205] Jones (2), p. 173.
[206] Camp, p. 51.
[207] Camp, p. 50.
[208] Notebook.

[209] Lee (2), p. 125.
[210] Lee (2), p. 125.
[211] Lee (2), p. 135.
[212] Lee (2), p. 133.
[213] Lee (2), p. 133.
[214] Lee (2), p. 137.
[215] Jones (2), p. 417.
[216] Jones (1), p. 468.
[217] Camp, p. 52.
[218] Moore, p. 10.
[219] Camp, p. 80.
[220] Pendleton (2), pp. 375-76.
[221] Lee (2), p. 143.
[222] Lee (2), p. 144.
[223] Lee (2), p. 146.
[224] Chautauquan, p. 189.
[225] Whipple, p. 179.
[226] Lee (2), p. 152.
[227] Lee (2), p. 149.
[228] Alexander, p. 600.
[229] Jones (2), p. 167.
[230] Page (1), p. 257.
[231] Lee (2), p. 153.
[232] Jones (2), p. 314.
[233] Jones (2), p. 43.
[234] Lee (1), p. 395.
[235] Jones (2), p. 308.
[236] White, p. 431.
[237] Jones (2), p. 195.
[238] Jones (2), p. 196.
[239] Lee (2), p. 172.

WHERE FOUND

[240] Jones (1), p. 201.
[241] Lee (2), p. 182.
[242] Lee (2), p. 185.
[243] Page (1), p. 649.
[244] White, p. 437.
[245] Faculty—in Riley, p. 39.
[246] Lee (2), p. 279.
[247] Lee (2), p. 189.
[248] Jones (2), p. 404.
[249] Joynes, p. 19.
[250] Moore, p. 11.
[251] Camp, p. 77.
[252] Riley (Rev. W. Strotter Jones quoted), p. 107. The Macmillan Company.
[253] Jones (2), p. 144.
[254] Lee (1), p. 417.
[255] McKim, p. 217. Longmans, Green & Co.
[256] Young, p. 344.
[257] Lee (2), p. 262.
[258] Lee (2), p. 236.
[259] Jones (2), p. 256.
[260] Jones (2), p. 252.
[261] Jones (2), p. 114.
[262] Jones (2), p. 111.
[263] Camp, p. 59.
[264] Camp, p. 60.
[265] Camp, p. 60.
[266] Jones (2), p. 113.
[267] Long, p. 462.
[268] Camp, p. 78.
[269] White, p. 456.

[270] Riley (David J. Wilson quoted), p. 133. The Macmillan Company.
[271] Long, p. 451.
[272] Camp, p. 78.
[273] Jones (2), p. 412.
[274] Jones (2), p. 323.
[275] Jones (2), p. 323.
[276] Jones (2), p. 114.
[277] Long, p. 485.
[278] Whipple, p. 77.
[279] Smith, p. 42.
[280] Outlook, p. 586.
[281] Jones (2), p. 197.
[282] Legion—in Bar, p. 18.
[283] Jones (2), p. 196.
[284] Jones (2), p. 174.
[285] Jones (2), p. 174.
[286] McKim, p. 180.
[287] Lee (1), p. 408.
[288] Long, p. 519.
[289] Jones (2), p. 176.
[290] Jones (2), p. 146.
[291] Jones (2), p. 177.
[292] Jones (2), p. 178.
[293] Lee (2), p. 231.
[294] Jones (2), p. 212.
[295] Lee (2), p. 224.
[296] Jones (2), p. 190.
[297] Jones (2), p. 190.
[298] Camp, p. 67.
[299] Camp, p. 67.

WHERE FOUND

[300] Camp, p. 71.
[301] Jones (2), p. 258.
[302] Lee (2), p. 260.
[303] Jones (2), p. 260.
[304] Lee (2), p. 336.
[305] Jones (2), p. 263.
[306] Lee (2), p. 303.
[307] Notebook.
[308] Lee (2), p. 297.
[309] Camp, p. 68.
[310] Lee (2), p. 352.
[311] Camp, p. 68.
[312] Jones (2), p. 170.
[313] Jones (2), p. 169.
[314] Jones (2), p. 169.
[315] Long, p. 31.
[316] Jones (2), p. 169.
[317] Jones (2), p. 170.
[318] Long, p. 29.
[319] Riley, p. 78.
[320] Long, p. 222.
[321] Jones (2), p. 165.
[322] Herald—in Jones (2), p. 63.
[323] Riley (Rev. Edward Clifford Gordon quoted), p. 78.
[324] Long, p. 451.
[325] Chautauquan, p. 189.
[326] Lee (2), p. 30.
[327] Jones (2), p. 480.
[328] Riley, p. 177.
[329] Chautauquan, p. 188.

[330] Moore, p. 11.
[331] Lee (2), p. 352.
[332] Lee (2), p. 362.
[333] Lee (2), p. 385.
[334] Lee (2), p. 386.
[335] Lee (2), p. 390.
[336] Lee (2), p. 405.
[337] Camp, p. 65.
[338] Moore, p. 11.
[339] Shepherd, p. 47.
[340] Camp, p. 66.
[341] Lee (2), p. 317.
[342] Camp, p. 78.
[343] Riley, p. 100.
[344] Riley, p. 38.
[345] Riley, p. 155.
[346] Riley, p. 100.
[347] Chautauquan, p. 100.
[348] Riley, p. 177.
[349] Jones (2), p. 458.
[350] Camp, p. 61.
[351] Camp, p. 61.
[352] Camp, p. 63.
[353] Camp, p. 64.
[354] Lee (2), p. 435.
[355] Lee (2), p. 435.
[356] Lee (2), p. 437.
[357] Lee (2), p. 438.
[358] McKim, p. 189.
[359] Shepherd, p. 48.
[360] Lee (2), p. 440.

WHERE FOUND

[361] Collegian—in Jones (2), p. 462.
[362] Jones (2), p. 454.
[363] Jones (2), p. 458.
[364] Mason, p. 383.
[365] Camp, p. 61.
[366] Riley (Rev. J. W. Jones quoted), p. 189.
[367] Young, p. 343.
[368] Jones (1), p. 444.
[369] Jones (1), p. 135.
[370] Jones (2), p. 56.
[371] Telegraph—in Jones (2), p. 71.
[372] Riley (Rev. Edward Clifford Gordon quoted), p. 78.
[373] Jones (2), p. 327.
[374] Jones (2), p. 464.
[375] Jones (2), p. 468.
[376] Lee (1), p. 424.
[377] Lee (2), p. 106.
[378] Jones (2), p. 341.
[379] Lee (2), p. 75.
[380] Camp, p. 81.
[381] Jones (2), p. 480.
[382] Lee (2), p. 475.
[383] Joynes, p. 19.
[384] Long, p. 66.
[385] White, p. 32.
[386] Mason, p. 381.
[387] Lee (2), p. 19.
[388] Smith, p. 5.
[389] Keyes, p. 20.
[390] Herald—in Jones (2), p. 63.

[391] Jones (1), p. 71.
[392] Smith, p. 5.
[393] Smith, p. 5.
[394] Wise, p. 342.
[395] Jones (2), p. 359.
[396] *Standard*—in Brock, p. 5.
[397] *Herald*—in Jones (2), p. 63.
[398] *Sun*—in Jones (2), p. 61.
[399] Blackwood—in Jones (2), p. 75.
[400] Veteran (John B. Collyar quoted), p. 265.
[401] Hosmer, p. 29.
[402] Wolseley, p. 5.
[403] Lee (1), p. 418.
[404] Bradford, p. 246.
[405] McKim, p. 209.
[406] Cooke, p. 2.
[407] McKim, p. 204.
[408] Jones (2), p. 428.
[409] Young, p. 344.
[410] Young, p. 345.
[411] McKim, p. 209.
[412] Hayne—Jones (2), p. 361.
[413] Keckley, p. 137.
[414] Hayne—Jones (2), p. 361.
[415] Bradford, p. 246.

NAMES OF THE DEITY

The terms one uses in referring to the Deity reveal his inner thought and conception of God and His attributes. In the quotations in this book, General Lee used *forty-five*.

In *Abraham Lincoln the Christian*, Lincoln used *forty-nine*.

In *George Washington the Christian*, Washington used *fifty-four*.

The page on which the name first occurs is given.

Almighty Hand	100
Christ	129
Divine Mercy	100
Father in Heaven	109
Heavenly Father	40
Merciful Father in Heaven	121
Giver of Victory	105
Giver of All Victory	92
Giver of All Victories	88
God	36
Almighty God	57
All-Wise God	137

    God of Battles.......................... 149
    God of Heaven.......................... 199
    God of Mercy and Truth................. 196
    God of Our Forefathers.................. 129
    Good God.............................. 41
    Great God.............................. 130
    Great God of Heaven.................... 86
    Kind God.............................. 50
    Merciful God........................... 50

Heaven................................... 147

Heavenly Creator.......................... 54

Heavenly Power........................... 112

Holy Spirit............................... 207

Lord..................................... 104
    Lord of Hosts.......................... 103
    Lord and Saviour....................... 124

Maker.................................... 83

Merciful Creator........................... 198

Most High................................ 81

Power.................................... 151

Providence................................ 52
    All-Wise Providence..................... 105
    Divine Providence...................... 53

NAMES OF THE DEITY 277

    Kind Providence.......................... 148
    Merciful Providence....................... 69
    Overruling Providence..................... 40
    Wise Providence.......................... 198

Redeemer.................................... 207

Ruler of the Universe........................ 82
    Great Ruler of the Universe............... 81
    Great Ruler of the World................. 195
    Sovereign Ruler of the Universe........... 94

Saviour...................................... 47

NOTES

In 1871, soon after the death of General Lee, the name of Washington College was changed to "The Washington and Lee University." In the same year General George Washington Custis Lee succeeded his father as president, and served in that capacity for twenty-six years (1871-1897).

Soon after the outbreak of the Civil War the work of the college was discontinued, most of the students enlisting in the Confederate Army. The buildings and other property were much injured when Lexington was occupied by the Federal Army in June, 1864.

In 1798, George Washington made a generous gift to the institution, then known as Liberty Hall Academy, and the name was changed to Washington Academy. In 1813 it was changed to Washington College. The property which Washington donated still yields an annual income of three thousand dollars.

During General Lee's administration of five years, the growth of the college in numbers and influence was phenomenal. In 1859-60 there were ninety-five students, all save one being registered from Virginia. In 1867-68 there were four hundred and ten students, representing twenty states and one foreign country, and sixty-eight per cent of them came from beyond the borders of Virginia. At the time of Lee's death, the enrollment had reached eight hundred.

"Traveller" was General Lee's famous war horse. Lee always used the old English spelling, with two l's.

LEE MEMORIAL CHAPEL

Behind the platform and visible from the body of the chapel is Valentine's recumbent statue of Lee. Below this, on the basement floor, is the crypt containing the body of (1) General Robert E. Lee; (2) his wife, Mary Custis Lee; (3) his father, General Henry Lee ("Light Horse Harry"), which was brought from Georgia to Virginia in May, 1913; (4) his mother, Anne Carter Lee; his three daughters, (5) Mary Custis, (6) Agnes, and (7) Mildred; his three sons, (8) General George Washington Custis Lee, (9) General William Harry Fitzhugh Lee, and (10) Captain Robert E. Lee, Jr.; and his grandson, (11) Robert E. Lee, III, son of W. H. Fitzhugh Lee. Besides these are the remains of (12) Mary Tabb Bolling, second wife of W. H. Fitzhugh Lee, and their three infant children, (13) (14) (15); also the remains of (16) Juliet Carter, second wife of Robert E. Lee, Jr. General Lee's daughter, Annie Custis, is buried at Warrenton Springs, Warren County, North Carolina.

General Lee had two brothers and two sisters, and a half-brother.

Washington and Lee were born in the same county.

Washington was the son of his father's second wife.
Lincoln was reared by his father's second wife.
Lee was the son of his father's second wife.

Each became a half-orphan at an early age:
Washington at the age of eleven—father died.
Lincoln at the age of nine—mother died.
Lee at the age of eleven—father died.

Washington died at the age of sixty-seven.
Lincoln was assassinated at the age of fifty-six.
Lee died at the age of sixty-three.

Mrs. Washington died two years after Mr. Washington, in 1801.
Mrs. Lincoln died seventeen years after Mr. Lincoln, in 1882.
Mrs. Lee died three years after Mr. Lee, in 1873.

Washington had no children—adopted two—son and daughter.
Lincoln had four children—sons.
Lee had seven children—three sons and four daughters.

ABRAHAM LINCOLN WAS A LEE

President Lincoln's great-grandmother was Nancy Lee. The late Rev. Dr. William E.

Barton, the best authority on the ancestry of Lincoln, after a long "hunt through musty records in the courthouses and garrets of Virginia," declares:

"It is my confident belief that the family of Lees from which Abraham Lincoln was descended was the same family from which Robert E. Lee was descended, both men being descendants of old Colonel Richard Lee." [Colonel Richard Lee was the beginning of the Lee family in America. He was the great-great-grandfather of Robert E. Lee.]

On February 25, 1895, a great-great-granddaughter of Joseph Hanks, Sr., the grandfather of Nancy Hanks Lincoln, mother of President Lincoln, wrote that the wife of Joseph Hanks, Sr., "was a Lucy [Nancy] Lee of Virginia, a relative of Robert E. Lee."

Were those two great leaders of opposing forces really cousins? Did "the proud blood of the Lees" flow through the veins of Lincoln?

Were these three men relatives, "The Great Triumvirate Among the Makers of America"?

Lee was related to Washington by marriage to the daughter of Washington's adopted son, the grandson of Mrs. Washington.

If Lincoln descended from the same family of Lees, then the family relationship is established.

INDEX

Headings in CAPITALS

A

ABANDON ANIMOSITIES, 17, 183
Acre, 21
Adams, President John Quincy, 33
Addresses to Army:
　Battle of Fredericksburg, 100
　Battle of Chancellorsville, 104
Alexander, General E. P., 151
ALEXANDRIA ACADEMY, 30
ALEXANDRIA, MOVES TO, 23
Alexandria, Virginia, 23, 24, 26, 28, 29, 31, 35, 41, 48, 49, 208
ALMIGHTY GOD, GRATEFUL TO, 94
"ALL THINGS FOR OUR GOOD," 122
"AM I A CHRISTIAN?" 213
Anderson, Colonel Archer, 150
Andersonville prisoners, 192
ANNIVERSARY OF WEDDING, 138
ANOTHER FUNERAL SERVICE, 54
APOSTOLIC SUCCESSION, 214
APPEAL, THE, 222
APPEARANCE, HIS, 68
Appomattox, 152, 154, 254
Arlington, Virginia, 34, 36, 41, 44, 46, 49, 55, 56, 57, 58, 60, 62, 63, 64, 68, 69, 70, 73, 87, 122
Ashby, T. A., 200
Atkinson, Rev. Dr. Thomas, 42

"Audley," Virginia, Mrs. Lee there, 79
Augusta, Georgia, 188

B

Baccalaureate Sermon, 171
Baltimore, Maryland, moved there, 42; wrote from, 43; oldest sister, 62; offered hat, 169; 197, 199
Baptist Church, Lexington, Virginia, 213
Barton, the Rev. Dr. William E., 280
Bath County, Virginia, Mrs. Lee there, 82
BATTLE NOT ALWAYS TO THE STRONG, 147
Battle of Brandy Station, 109
BATTLE OF CHANCELLORSVILLE, 104
BATTLE OF COLD HARBOR, 93
BATTLE OF FREDERICKSBURG, 100
BATTLE OF GETTYSBURG, 112
BATTLE OF MANASSAS, 78
Battle of the Wilderness, 108
"BEAU-IDEAL OF A CHRISTIAN," 35
BENEFIT FUND, REFUSES, 190
BEST THING IN THE WORLD, THE, 215
BIBLE, ACCEPTS CHAPEL, 169
BIBLE, GIFT OF, 165
BIBLE, LOVE FOR, 217
BIBLE, POCKET, 231
BIBLE, STOLEN, 168
BIBLE SOCIETY, PRESIDENT OF, 218
Bible Society, Rockbridge, 218, 219, 222

283

INDEX

Bible Society, Virginia, 194, 224
BITTER EXPRESSIONS, OMIT, 183
BITTERNESS, NO, 110
BLACKWOOD'S MAGAZINE, 247
Blair, Francis P., interview with, 60; interview referred to, 66; Lee's words to, 67
BLESSING AT THE TABLE, 145
Blue Ridge, slept on top of, 161
BOARD OF TRUSTEES, REFUSES OFFER FROM, 188
BOARD OF TRUSTEES, REPORT TO, 180
BOOKS, TWO FAVORITE, 217
"BOYS, MY DEAR," 39
BOY, THE, 28
BRANDY, CARRIED THROUGH THE WAR, 201
Brantly, the Rev. Dr. W. T., 206
BRANTLY, THE REV. DR. W. T., 239
Broadus, the Rev. Dr. John A., 171
Brooklyn, New York, 196
BROWN, CAPTURE OF JOHN, 55
Brown, the Rev. Dr. William, 164
Bunker Hill, Virginia, 115
BURIAL, 230
BURIAL SERVICE, PERFORMS, 53
Butler, General Benjamin F., 123, 125

C

Calvary, Cross of, 67
Cameron, Secretary of War, 60
Camp Brown, Texas, 50, 52
Camp Cooper, Texas, 50, 53, 54
Camp Culpeper, 116

Camp near Fredericksburg, 97
Camp on Sewell's Mountain, 83
Camp Orange Court House, 121, 130
Camp Petersburg, 137, 138
Camp Rapidan, 122
Camp Rappahannock, 121
Camp Valley Mountain, 79
CAPTURE OF JOHN BROWN, 55
CAREFUL IN CONVERSATION, 35
CARTERS, THE, 22
Carter, Anne Hill, Lee's mother, 22, 279
Carter, Charles, 23
Carter, Robert, 22
Carterville, Virginia, 158
CASTS LOT WITH VIRGINIA, 64
Central Presbyterian, 164
"Chaffins," 146
Chambersburg, Pennsylvania, order to army, 110
CHAPEL BIBLE, ACCEPTS, 169
CHAPEL SERVICES, 170
Chaplain, college, 168; invites ministers, 170
Chaplains' Association, 126
CHAPLAINS, INTEREST IN WORK OF, 135
Chesney, Colonel Charles Cornwallis, 17
Childe, Mrs. Edward Vernon, death of, 50
CHILDREN, LOVE FOR, 76
CHILDREN'S COMPANION, 42
CHOICE, HIS, 62
CHRISTIAN:
  Beau-ideal of a Christian, 35
  Christian faith, 49
  Christian nations, 51
  Christian burial, 54
  Christian letter, 71

284

INDEX

Classed among Christians, 71
Bear trials like Christians, 74
Christian civilization, 110
Christianity, 11, 114, 238, 250, 252
Devout Christian, 119
Christian commander, 120
Humble, earnest Christian, 127
Sustained by the Christian's faith and hope, 137
A Christian man, 151
Final test of a true Christian, 157
Make Christian men, 163
Become real Christians, 164
A sincere Christian, 164
Importance of the Christian religion, 171
Good Christians, 176
Special aim to feel a Christian, 213
His chief concern to be a Christian, 214
A Christian gentleman, 215
Christian people, 239
Making them sincere Christians, 240
A noble Christian, 245
As devout a Christian, 246
A sincere Christian, 246
Christian without hypocrisy, 248
True Christian discipleship, 253
The Christian gentleman, 254
"CHRISTIAN, AM I A?" 213
"CHRISTIAN, BEAU-IDEAL OF A," 35
CHRISTIAN CHARACTER, SUMMARY OF, 215
CHRISTIAN CHARITY, 155

Christian commission, 139
CHRISTIAN SPIRIT OF FORGIVENESS, 181
"Christian, Was He a?" 95
CHRISTMAS, 1856, 52
CHRISTMAS DAY, 1861, TO WIFE ON, 86
CHRISTMAS DAY, 1861, TO DAUGHTER ON, 87
CHRISTMAS FAMILY PARTY, 1861, 86
CHRISTMAS DAY, 1862, 99
CHURCH, BECOMES MEMBER OF, 48
Church, Christ, Alexandria, Virginia, Lee's mother member, 26; Lee worshiped, 28; helped decorate, 28; confirmed, 48; children baptized, 49; agrees to take command Virginia forces, 64; letter to pastor, 71
CHURCH, LEE AND JACKSON AT, 103
CHURCH, LITTLE GIRL IN, WITH GENERAL LEE, 140
CHURCH WORK, ACTIVE IN, 212
CHURCHES:
Baptist Church, Lexington, Virginia, 171, 213, 229, 238
Christ Church, Alexandria, Virginia, 26, 28, 48, 49, 64, 71
Christ Church, Lancaster County, Virginia, 23
Church of Fort Hamilton, New York Harbor, 37
First Presbyterian, Richmond, Virginia, 106
First Presbyterian, Nashville, Tennessee, 106, 240
Grace Church, Lexington, Virginia, 145, 208
Methodist Church, Lexington, Virginia, 171

INDEX

Presbyterian Church, Lexington, Virginia, 164, 171, 225, 230
Saint George's Chapel, 22
Saint Paul's Church, Baltimore, Maryland, 197
Saint Paul's Church, Richmond, Virginia, 155
Saint Peter's Church, Baltimore, Maryland, 42
Saint Peter's Church, New Kent, Virginia, 209
Saint Thomas Church, New York City, 164
CHURCHES, DESTRUCTION OF, 138
CHURCHES, REGULAR ATTENDANT AT COUNTRY, 158
Clarke County, Virginia, Mrs. Lee there, 79
Clarke, J. L., 222
CLEAN IN SPEECH, 204
Cocke, Captain Edmund Randolph, 158
COLD HARBOR, BATTLE OF, 92, 93
Cole, the Rev. Mr., 139
COLLEGE CHAPEL, THE, 167
COLLEGE PRESIDENT, THE, 161
COLLEGE PRESIDENT AND A LITTLE CHILD, 174
Collyar, John B., 247
COMFORT IN SORROW, 199
COMMAND OF U. S. ARMY, OFFERED, 65
Commander-in-Chief, appointed, 147
"CONCERT OF PRAYER FOR COLLEGES," 206
CONFEDERATE VETERAN, 247
Confirmed, 48
Connecticut, legislature of, 44
Contributions, 212
Coosawhatchie, South Carolina, 85
COUNSEL TO HIS SON, 43

Crowning glory, 251
Culpeper Court House, 139
Cumberland, Georgia, father's grave, 87
Custis, Mrs., 209
Custis, George W. P., father of Mrs. Lee, 34; Mrs. Lee lived in home, 50; death, 55; *Recollections of George Washington*, 78; leaves farm to grandson, 90; frees slaves, 103
Custis, Mrs. George W. P., Mrs. Lee's mother, 46
Custis, Mary Randolph, married to Robert E. Lee, 34
Custis, Nellie, aunt of Mrs. Lee, 103

D

Dana, Charles A., 246
Dana, the Rev. Charles B., baptized Lee's children, 49
DAUGHTERS, TO HIS, 79
"DAUGHTERS, MY DARLING," 85
DAUGHTER'S GRAVE, DESIRES TO VISIT, 209
DAUGHTER'S GRAVE, VISITS, 210
DAUGHTER, MONUMENT AT GRAVE OF, 158
DAUGHTER ON THE DEATH OF HER FATHER, TO, 197
DAUGHTER-IN-LAW, DEATH OF, 123; letters to, 133
DAUGHTER-IN-LAW, TO HIS NEW, 197
Daughter-in-law and family prayers, 205
DAVIS, JEFFERSON, 237
Davis, President Jefferson, Lee adviser to, 85; prayer for, 88; promotes Lee, 90; Lee reports to, 92; appoints fast day, 102; dispatch to,

INDEX

104; appoints day of fasting, 117; another fast day, 129; escape, 148; in prison, 192, 195
DAVIS, JEFFERSON, RELEASED FROM PRISON, 195
DEATH OF BISHOP MEADE, 90
DEATH OF COLONEL WASHINGTON, 83
DEATH OF DAUGHTER ANNIE, 96
Death of father, 24
DEATH OF FATHER, TO DAUGHTER ON THE, 197
DEATH OF GENERAL STUART, 136
DEATH OF GRANDDAUGHTER, 97
DEATH OF MOTHER, 34
DEATH OF MRS. HOGE, 194
DEATH OF MRS. LEE'S FATHER, 55
DEATH OF MRS. LEE'S MOTHER, 46
DEATH OF SON, TO FATHER ON ACCIDENTAL, 197
DEATH OF SON, TO MOTHER ON ACCIDENTAL, 197
DEATH OF "STONEWALL" JACKSON, 105
DEATH OF YOUNGEST SISTER, 50
DECLINED SPECIAL EXCHANGE FOR HIS SON, 131
DELEGATE TO EPISCOPAL CONVENTION, 208
Ditchley, estate of, 22
Dobb's Farm, 94
Doubts, religious, 49
Drunkenness, at West Point, 33; in the war, 202
Dudley, the Rev. Thomas U., 95
Dungeness, Georgia, burial place of Lee's father, 87
DUST, KNEELS IN, 140

DUTY, ALL-COMPELLING SENSE OF, 67
DUTY, FRANKNESS AND, 44
Duty, sublimest word, 45; path of, 61; of an American citizen, 63; ideal of, 161; keynote, 162

E

Earl of Litchfield, 21
Early, General J. A., 153
Easter, 155
EASTER SERVICE IN HIS TENT, 52
EDUCATION, HIS IDEAL OF, 163
EFFECT OF THE ORDER, 118
Elliott, Bishop, prayer for President, 88; death, 193
ELLIOTT, LETTER OF COMFORT TO MRS., 193
Engineer Corps or Department, 34, 35, 72
Episcopal catechism, taught by mother, 26; recited to Bishop Meade, 26, 90, 91
Episcopal Church, Lee baptized, 26; becomes member, 48; consistent member, 79
EPISCOPAL CONVENTION, ATTENDS, 73
EPISCOPAL CONVENTION, DELEGATE TO, 208
EPISCOPAL SERVICE, ATTENDS, 40
Episcopal Theological Seminary, 35
Essex, estate in, 21
Eveleth, James, testimony, 35
Everett's *Life of Washington*, 59
"EVERYBODY LOVES COLONEL LEE," 42
EVOLUTION, 108

INDEX

F

FACING THE ISSUE, 60
Fairfax Court House, 73
Family moves to Arlington, 49
FAMILY MOVES TO RICHMOND, LEE'S, 92
Family prayers, punctual, 45
Farrar, Colonel F. R., 169
FAST DAY, 102
FASTING AND PRAYER, 88
FASTING, DAY OF, 117, 129
FASTING DURING LENT, 215
FATHER, A LOVING, 92
FATHER, HIS, 23
FATHER, MERCIFUL, 109
FATHER ON ACCIDENTAL DEATH OF SON, TO, 198
FATHER'S GRAVE, VISITS, 87
Fauquier County, Virginia, Mrs. Lee there, 74
FAVORITE BOOKS, TWO, 217
FAVORITE HYMNS, HIS, 217
FOOTSTEPS, IN HIS FATHER'S, 35
FORGIVENESS, CHRISTIAN SPIRIT OF, 181
FORGIVENESS OF GOD, IMPLORES, 103
Fort Hamilton, New York Harbor, 37, 39
Fort Mason, Texas, 52, 59
Fort of Perote, Mexico, 40
Fortress Monroe, 34, 35, 116, 132, 133, 195
Fredericksburg, Camp, 97, 98, 99, 101, 102, 105
Fredericksburg, Virginia, meeting in, 103; Episcopal convention, 208
Friend, one intimate, 254
FUNERAL SERVICE, ANOTHER, 54
Furloughs, requested by Jews, 79, 80, 144

G

GAMBLING, 76
GENTLEMAN:
  Most manly and entire gentleman, 68
  A Christian gentleman, 215
  Test of a true gentleman, 232
  Most chivalrous gentleman, 233
  Lofty dignity of the Christian gentleman, 233
  Highest type of Christian gentleman, 233
  Model of an upright gentleman, 236
  A nobler gentleman, 246
  The Christian gentleman, 254
GENTLEMAN, A CHRISTIAN, 233
GENTLEMAN, TEST OF A TRUE, 232
Gethsemane, 67
GETHSEMANE, LEE'S, 148
Gettysburg, Pennsylvania, wounded soldier, 113; reproves officer, 203
GIVER OF ALL VICTORIES, 88
GIVER OF ALL VICTORY, 98
GOD'S ALMIGHTY ARM, 130
GOD'S BEAUTIFUL WORLD, 109
God, cardinal fact, 254
GODFATHER TO GRANDSON, 208
GOD, HOPE IN, 121
GOD, IMPLORES FORGIVENESS OF, 115
GOD IN HIS HEART, 250, 232
GOD, IN THE HANDS OF, 50
God, intimate friend, 254
GOD, LEAVE RESULTS TO, 165
"GOD, NOT REPINE AT WILL OF," 117

INDEX

God, Reliance Upon, 75
God's Mercy, Realization of, 207
God's Will Be Done, 105
God's Will, Resigned to, 69
God's Will, Submit to, 114
Gordon, Rev. Edward Clifford, 203
Grace Church, Lexington, Virginia, 145, 208, 225, 230
"Grand Military Ball," 135
Grandson, Godfather to, 208
Grant, General, 140, 147, 150, 183
Grateful to Almighty God, 94
Gratitude to Heavenly Father, 93
Grave, Visits Father's, 87
Great in Defeat, 152
Great Ruler of the Universe, 81
Greene, General Nathanael, 24
Grief, His Great, 132
Grieves Over Loss of Men, 137
Grogshops, Close, 201

H

Habits, 30
Hafiz, 182
Hagerstown, Maryland, 112
Hallowell, Benjamin, teacher of Lee, 31
Hamilton's Crossing, 140
Hampton, General Wade, 67
"Happiness, What is?" 24
Harper's Ferry, 55
Hat, Refuses Gift of, 169
Hatcher's Run, 141
Heavenly Father, Gratitude to, 94

Hebrew Congregation, Richmond, Virginia, 80
Heth, General Gordon, 141
"Hickory Hill," wounded son there, 109; son captured, 116
Hill, General A. P., 108, 141
Hill, Senator Benjamin, 248
Hilliard, Hon. H. W., 188
His Great Mistake, 215
Hoge, Death of Mrs., 194
Hoge, the Rev. Dr. Moses D., 194
Holland, the Rev. R. A., memorial address, 18
Home of Lee, The, 55
Home, His Return, 155
Home, His Wife Driven from, 70
Home in a Quiet Spot, Longs for, 196
Home, Loss of, 87
Home, Urges Wife to Leave, 70
Honesty, 70, 246
Hope, Hon. A. W. Beresford, 165
Hot Springs, Virginia, Mrs. Lee there, 82
Hour Had Come, The Appointed, 226
"Human Virtue equal to Human Calamity," 153
Humane Commander, A, 110
Hunt, General Henry J., 36, 242
Hunterville, West Virginia, 78
Hymn, His Favorite, 217

I

Ideal Man, The, 254
Immorality, avoid, 56
Immoral language, avoided, 32, 35, 247, 252

289

INDEX

IMPLORES FORGIVENESS OF GOD, 113
INFLUENCE OF YOUNG MAN'S LIFE, 31
INTEREST IN WELFARE OF MEN, 134
INTEREST IN WORK OF CHAPLAINS, 135
IN THE HANDS OF GOD, 50
Intoxicating liquor, avoided, 30, 32
"IS IT RIGHT?" 150

J

JACKSON AT CHURCH, LEE AND, 103
Jackson, General "Stonewall," letter to, 98; headquarters, 103; prayers, 107; his chaplain, 126; preaching at headquarters, 136; pastor, 164; headquarters, 205, 228, 229, 244, 245
JACKSON, "STONEWALL," WOUNDED, 103
JACKSON, "STONEWALL," DEATH OF, 105
Jeffersonton, Virginia, 94
JEWISH RABBI, LETTER TO, 80
Jewish soldier, application of, 79
Joannes, Count, letter to, 155
Johns, Bishop John, confirmed Lee, 48
Johnson, the Hon. Reverdy, letter to, 65
Johnston, General Albert Sidney, 225
JOHNSTON, COLONEL WILLIAM PRESTON, 236
Johnston, Colonel William P., 225, 230
Johnstone, Mrs. [W. J.], visits Lexington, Virginia, 13

JOINED IN PRAYER, 148
JONES, MISS ANN UPSHUR, TO, 196
Jones, the Rev. Mr., 175
Jones, Rev. J. William, Chaplain, the Lee family, 56; fast day services, 118; "noble Christian leader," 120; Sabbath Observance, 126; Lee's self-denial, 134; Lee at service, 140; prayer-books, 141; results of war, 165; Lee and Bibles, 166; revivals, 180; notes, 183; "old soldier," 184; "no unkind word," 193; grogshops, 201; Lee at services, 205; address, 206; God's mercy, 207; revival in colleges, 208; contribution, 213; assisted at Lee's funeral, 229; pocket Bible, 231; finds Lee's notes, 232
JONES, THE REV. DR. J. WILLIAM, 238
Jones, the Rev. W. Strother, 164
JOYNES, PROFESSOR EDWARD S., 241

K

Keith, the Rev. Dr. Ruel, married Robert E. Lee, 35
Kentucky Military Institute, memorial address, 21; revival, 207
KEY NOTE OF HIS LIFE, THE, 162
Key to his character, 251
King George, 61
"Kinlock," Virginia, Mrs. Lee there, 74
Kirkpatrick, the Rev. Dr. Thomas J., conversation, 176
KNEELS IN THE DUST, 140

INDEX

L

Lacy, the Rev. B. T., conducts service, 104; interviews Lee, 126
LAST ORDER TO THE ARMY, 154
LAST PUBLIC ACT, HIS, 225
LAST WORDS, 227
Lawton, General, 242
Leary, W. B., Lee's teacher, 30
LEAVE RESULTS TO GOD, 165
LEE AND JACKSON AT CHURCH, 103
Lee coat-of-arms, 22
"LEE, EVERYBODY LOVES COLONEL," 42
Lee Memorial Chapel, 167, 279
Lee monument, 150
LEE, ROBERT E., birth, 23; baptism, 26; catechism, 26; learned Bible, 27; worshiped, 28; decorated church, 28; habits, 30; Alexandria Academy, 30; letter to teacher, 30; never censured, 30; exemplary student, 31; influence, 31; at West Point, 32; never reprimanded, 32; cared for dying mother, 34
LEE, ROBERT E., lieutenant, 34; first lieutenant, 36; captain, 36; colonel, 41; lieutenant-colonel, 49; major-general, 65; commander-in-chief, 147
LEE, ROBERT E., marriage, 34; vestryman, 37; superintendent of West Point, 45; member of church, 48; executor father-in-law's will, 55; resignation, 61; frees slaves, 100; tomb, 279; relative of Lincoln, 280; relative of Washington, 281
LEE, ROBERT E., at Fortress Monroe, 34; Saint Louis, 35; Fort Hamilton, 37; Mexican War, 39; Baltimore, 42; Arlington, 44; West Point, 45; Texas, 49; Arlington, 55; Texas, 58; Arlington, 60; Richmond, 65; Virginia military forces, 65; West Virginia, 78; Richmond, 85; South Carolina, 85; Georgia, 87; Richmond, 90; Confederate forces, 90; Army of Northern Virginia, 92; Pennsylvania, 110; Maryland, 112; Virginia, 115
LEE, ROBERT E., AND THE BIBLE:
His mother taught him, 27
Belief in the Bible, 49
Christmas story, 52
Gift of four volumes, 76
Supply the army, with Bibles rather than bullets, 120
Quoted, 156
Gift from English admirers, 165
"Accept it as the infallible Word of God," 166
His Bible stolen, 168
Accepts gift of Bible for college chapel, 169
No one too old to study the Bible, 179
Virginia Bible Society, 194
Bible and family prayer, 206
Read Bible every day in army, 217
Tried to circulate Bible among soldiers, 217
His favorite book, 217

INDEX

President of Bible Society, 218
Appeal for funds to buy Bibles, 222
Interested in Virginia Bible Society, 224
His pocket Bible, 231
LEE, ROBERT E., AT CHURCH AND PRAYER:
Baptized in Episcopal Church, 26
Worshiped in Christ Church, Alexandria, 28
Member of vestry, Fort Hamilton, New York, 37
Attends Episcopal service, Fort Perote, Mexico, 40
Sunday service at West Point, 46
Becomes member of Christ Church, Virginia, 48
Goes to church, Camp Brown, Texas, Christmas, 1856, 52
Easter service in his tent, Fort Mason, Texas, 53
Read funeral service, 53
Read funeral service again, 54
Helps build church, 58
A night of prayer, 61
Decision at Christ Church, Alexandria, Virginia, 64
Attends Episcopal Convention, 73
Religious tolerance, 79
Fasting and prayer, at church, 88
Attends service in Brigade, 92
Lee and Jackson at church, 103
Prays for "Stonewall" Jackson, 104
Lee and Jackson attend prayers, 107
Joins ragged veterans in prayer, 108
Forbids disturbance of prayer meeting, 108
Took part in camp prayer meeting, 119
Ardent in worship, 120
Prayer for nephews, 121
Visitor at chaplain's meetings, 135
Always attended preaching, 136
Rides to Richmond for early Sunday morning service, 136
Divine service under the trees, 137
Kept from church, 139
Destruction of churches, 139
Little girl beside him in church, 140
Kneels in dust, 141
Thankful for prayers, 143
Blessing at table, 145
Prays daily, 147
Joined in prayer, 148
Easter at church, 155
Prayed for enemies, 157
Attended Saint Paul's Church, Richmond, 157
Attended country churches, 158
Obtained college chapel, 167
Attended morning prayers, 167
Preferred simple, practical sermons, 171
Wanted prayers not too long, 172
Regular attendant at church, 173
Always knelt during prayer, 174
Wanted students to be Christians, 176

INDEX

Devout personal piety, 176
Interested in revivals, 180
Regular hours of prayer, 205
Family prayers every morning, 205
Responses in prayer, 206
Pray for revival, 207
Member vestry of Grace Church, Lexington, Virginia, 208
Delegate to Episcopal Council, 208
Godfather in baptism of grandson, 208
Active in church work, 212
Liberal contributor, 212
"A word in season," 213
"Abstain from special sins," 214
Best way to fast, 215
Presides at vestry meeting, 225
Unable to say grace at the table, 227

LEE, ROBERT E., LETTERS OF:
To his wife, 36, 40, 46, 50, 52, 53, 54, 58, 68, 69, 70, 72, 73, 74, 78, 79, 82, 83, 84, 86, 88, 90, 91, 94, 96, 99, 101, 105, 109, 114, 115, 117, 121, 122, 124, 137, 138, 147, 161, 162, 208
To his daughter, Agnes Lee, 102
To his daughter, Ann Carter Lee, 86, 89
To his daughter, Mary Custis Lee, 97
To his daughter, Mildred Lee, 85, 89, 99, 137, 209
To daughter on Christmas Day, 87
To his daughters, 79
To "My Darling Daughters," 85
To his daughter-in-law, 95, 98, 110, 116
To his new daughter-in-law, 197
To his son, George Washington Parke Custis Lee, 43, 44, 58, 59, 81
To his son, William H. Fitzhugh Lee, 39, 56, 57, 131, 132, 133, 163, 196, 199, 210
To his son, Robert E. Lee, Jr., 168
To "My Dear Boys," 39
To his oldest sister, Mrs. Anne R. Marshall, 62
To his brother, Captain Sydney Smith Lee, 41, 63
To a lady cousin, 40
To a cousin, Miss Margaret Stuart, 130
To daughter on the death of her father, 197
To father on accidental death of son, 198
To mother on accidental death of son, 198
To his pastor, the Rev. Cornelius Walker, 71
To Jewish Rabbi, 80, 144
To Lexington ministers, 170
To the Rev. Dr. Moses D. Hoge, 194
To the Rev. Dr. T. V. Moore, 143
To Baltimore friends, 169
To Count Joannes, 155
To invitation committee, 158
To Jefferson Davis, 195
To Mrs. Jefferson Davis, 192
To Mrs. Stephen Elliott, 193

INDEX

To Colonel F. R. Farrar, 169
To Hon. A. W. Beresford Hope, 165
To General "Stonewall" Jackson, 98
To Samuel R. George, 199
To Hon. Reverdy Johnson, 65
To Miss Ann Upshur Jones, 196
To Mrs. George R. Randolph, 193
To the Hon. A. J. Requier, 168
To Young Men's Christian Association, 178
To young officers, 135
Lee, Agnes, daughter, letter to, 102; accompanies father, 209, 211; tomb, 279
Lee, Anne, sister, delicate, 28
Lee, Anne Hill Carter, mother, 22; tomb, 279
Lee, Anne Carter, daughter, letters to, 86, 89; death, 96; monument erected, 97; monument unveiled, 158; last hymn, 158; visit to grave, 209, 210
Lee, Charles Carter, brother, 24, 28
Lee, Fitzhugh, nephew, tribute, 237
Lee, George Washington Parke Custis, oldest son, in father's footsteps, 36; at Fort Hamilton, 37; letter to, 39; counsel to, 43; frankness and duty, 44; letters to, 58, 59; letter from, 70; decide for himself, 81; letter to, 123; offered to be substitute, 132; father's sickness, 227; tomb, 279
Lee, Launcelot, 21

Lee, Lionel, 21
Lee, Major-General Henry, wife of, 23, 210; father of Robert E., 23; goes to West Indies, 24; death, 24; burial, 24; letter of, 24; Robert visits grave, 87; tomb, 279
Lee, Mary Custis, daughter, at Fort Hamilton, 37; letter to, 97; tomb, 279
Lee, Mildred, daughter, at school in Winchester, Virginia, 85; "sweet sixteen," 89; at school in North Carolina, 99; letters to, 137, 209; tomb, 279
Lee, Mildred, sister, 28
Lee, Mrs. Robert E., marriage, 34; at Fort Hamilton, 37; moves to Baltimore, 42; moves to West Point, 45; death of mother, 46; moves to Arlington, 49; sick, 52; death of father, 55; account of Lee's decision, 61; still at Arlington, 70; went to "Ravensworth," 73; went to "Kinloch," 74; edited *Recollections*, &c., 78; staying at "Audley," at Hot Springs, Virginia, 82; an invalid, 84; knit socks, 84; missed husband's visit, 85; at "White House," 90; moves to Richmond, 92; owned slaves, 101; slaves set free, 101; declines gift of annuity, 190; tomb, 279
Lee, Robert E., Jr., youngest son, early impression of father, 42; father punctual, 45; wants to enlist, 82; enters army, 91; loving father, 92; visited family, 93; keynote of father's life,

INDEX

162; his farm, 168; at chapel with father, 167; tribute to father, 242; tomb, 279

Lee, Sydney Smith, brother, in navy, 28; tells him of home-coming, 41; writes to him of resignation, 63; commodore in Confederate Navy, 64; funeral, 208; father of Fitzhugh, 237

Lee, William H. Fitzhugh, second son, at Fort Hamilton, 37; letter tò, 39; letters to, 56, 57; home, 90; home burned, 92; wounded, 109; captured, 116, 131; refused visit to sick wife, 123, 132; death of wife, 123; return from prison, 133; letters to, 163, 197; second wife, 197; letter to, 199, 210; child baptized, 208; tomb, 279

Leesburg, Virginia, prayers, 108

LEE'S SOLDIERS, 234

LENT, FASTING DURING, 215

LETTER, UNPUBLISHED, 71

Lewis, Mrs. Lorenzo, Mrs. Lee staying with, 79

Lexington Gazette, 222

Lexington, Virginia, 153, 159, 161

Leyburn, the Rev. Dr. George W., 103

LIFE GLIDING AWAY, 162

Life of Washington, 58

"Light Horse Harry," 23, 210

Lincoln, Abraham, tribute to mother, 27; inauguration, 59; offers command of U. S. Army to Lee, 60; in prayer, 62; messenger to Lee, 66, 67; "may fall," 72; "let 'em up easy," 154; assassination, 155; tribute to Lee, 253; relative of Lee, 280

LINCOLN, ASSASSINATION OF, 155

Lincoln, Captain Robert, 254

LINCOLN'S TRIBUTE TO GENERAL LEE, ABRAHAM, 253

LINCOLN WOULD DO, WHAT, 153

Logan, J. L., 200

"London Dock," 202

LONDON STANDARD, 245

Long, Colonel Armistead Lindsay, 92, 203

LOSING HIS TEMPER, 203

LOVES A JOKE, 40

Lynchburg, Virginia, 208

M

MAJESTIC PERSONALITY, 253

MANASSAS, BATTLE OF, 78, 95

MANSION IN RICHMOND, DECLINES, 122

MARRIAGE, 34

"Marse Robert," 109

Marshall, Chief Justice, 226

Marshall, Mrs. Anne R., oldest sister, 62

Marshall, Judge William L., 62

Massaponax, 141

May, Colonel, 57

McCarty, Mr., minister, 40

Meade, Bishop, catechism, 26; visits General Lee, 72; sermon, 73; sends for Lee, 90; death, 90, 226

MEADE, DEATH OF BISHOP, 90

Meade, General, 107

Meigs, General Montgomery C., 35, 242

MEMORIAL MEETINGS, 231

Memorial windows, 157

MEN, WILL NOT SACRIFICE HIS, 152

INDEX

Merciful Father, 109
Methodist Church, Lexington, Virginia, 171
Mexico, City of, 40
Mexico, returns from, 48
Mexican War, 36, 40, 41, 201, 202
Michelbacher, Rabbi M. J., 80, 144
Miller, S. G. M., 200
Mine Run, 107
Ministers:
  The Rev. Dr. Thomas Atkinson, 42
  The Rev. Dr. W. T. Brantly, 206, 239
  The Rev. Dr. John A. Broadus, 171
  The Rev. Dr. William Brown, 164
  The Rev. Mr. Cole, 139
  The Rev. Charles B. Dana, 49
  Bishop Stephen Elliott, 88, 193
  The Rev. Dr. Moses D. Hoge, 194
  The Rev. Edward Clifford Gordon, 203
  The Rev. R. A. Holland, 18
  Bishop John Johns, 48
  The Rev. Mr. Jones, 175
  The Rev. Dr. J. William Jones (see "Jones, the Rev. J. William")
  The Rev. W. Strother Jones, 164
  The Rev. Dr. Reuel Keith, 35
  The Rev. Dr. Thomas J. Kirkpatrick, 176
  The Rev. B. T. Lacy, 104, 126
  The Rev. Dr. George W. Leyburn, 103
  Mr. McCarty, 40
  Rabbi M. J. Michelbacher, 80, 144
  Bishop William Meade, 26, 72, 73, 90, 226
  The Rev. Dr. T. V. Moore, 106, 239
  The Rev. Dr. W. N. Pendleton, 145, 219, 222, 226, 229, 230
  Mr. Platt, 137, 138
  The Rev. Cornelius Walker, 71
  Bishop Whipple, 199
  The Rev. Dr. W. S. White, 162, 164, 229
  Bishop Joseph P. B. Wilmer, 75, 159
  The Rev. George Woodbridge, 224
  The Rev. Doctor ——, 156
Mistake, His Great, 215
Mitchell, John H., 233
Monument at Grave of Daughter, 158
Moore, The Rev. Dr. T. V., 239; memorial address, 104
Morals, 253
Mother, Death of, 34
Mother, Death of Mrs. Lee's, 46
Mother, Devotion to, 28
Mother, His, 26; overwatchful, 25; communicant Episcopal Church, 26; prayers, 27; at "Ravensworth," 34; last sickness, 34
Mother on Accidental Death of Son, to, 198
Mother's Girlhood Home, Visits, 210
Mount Vernon, 55, 83
"My Dear Boys," 39

N

Nassau, West Indies, 24
Natural Bridge, Virginia, 177
New Kent, Virginia, 209

INDEX

New York Herald, 246
New York Sun, 246
Nine Mile Road, 94
Norfolk, Virginia, 156, 202
North Carolina, White Sulphur Springs, 97

O

Orders to Army:
  Seven Days' Battles, 93
  Sabbath Observance, 94, 128
  Fast Day, 102
  Death of "Stonewall" Jackson, 105
  Chambersburg, Pennsylvania, 110
  Following Battle of Gettysburg, 112
  Day of Fasting, 117
  Last Order to the Army, 154
Ordinance of Secession, 64

P

Palm Sunday, 150
Pamunkey River, Virginia, 90, 92
Paris, France, death of sister, 50
"Passing Over the River," 228
Paying Taxes, 115
Peace Impossible, 68
Pendleton, General William Nelson, 145, 219, 226, 229, 230
Performs Burial Service, 53
Perote, Fort, 40
Petersburg, Virginia, 137, 138, 140, 141, 148
Pew in church and chapel, 174
Phillips, Wendell, 100
Pickett, Mrs., Lee's remark to father, 55

Pilgrim Fathers, 32
Platt, Mr., preaching, 137, 138
Pocket Bible, 231
Pratt, J. W., 222
Prayer, A Man of, 205
Prayer Book, a favorite, 217
Prayer Books, Tracts and, 141
Prayer, Daily, 147
Prayer, Fasting and, 88
Prayer for Colleges, Concert of, 206
Prayer for Nephews, 121
Prayer, Joined in, 148
Prayer Meeting, Will Not Disturb, 108
Prayers, Attends, 107
Prayers, Family, 205
Prayers, Liked Appropriate, 172
Prayers, Thankful for, 143
Praying on the Eve of Battle, 107
Preaching, Always Attended, 136
Presbyterian Church, First, Nashville, Tennessee, 104, 131
Presbyterian Church, First, Richmond, Virginia, 104
Presbyterian Church, Lexington, Virginia, 164
Presbyterian community, 197
President of Washington College, Elected, 159
President, the College, 161
Presidency, Reason for Accepting, 163
Preston, Colonel J. T. L., 219, 222
Preston, General John S., 242
Preston, General William, 231
Profanity, 204
Prospect Hill, Georgia, 192

297

INDEX

PUBLIC ACT, LAST, 225
PURITY AND VIRTUE, 57

Q

Quirk, E. J., 193

R

Randolph, General George W., 193
"Ravensworth," Virginia, Lee's mother died there, 34; Lee's wife staying there, 73
REBUKES CRITIC OF GENERAL GRANT, 183
Recollections of George Washington, 78
"Reconstruction Acts," 181
REFUSES BENEFIT FUND, 190
Refuses financial offers, 186
REFUTES SLANDER, 193
RELIANCE UPON GOD, 75
RELIGIOUS EXAMPLE, 173
RELIGIOUS TOLERANCE, 69
Requier, the Hon. A. J., 168
RESIGNATION, HIS, 62
RESIGNED TO GOD'S WILL, 69
REVERSES NECESSARY FOR CORRECTION, 89
REVIVAL IN ARMY, GREAT, 119
REVIVALS, 180
REVIVALS PROMOTED, 119
REWARD OF THE RIGHTEOUS, 193
Richard Coeur de Lion, 21
Richmond, Virginia, 65, 66, 68, 69, 71, 72, 74, 76, 79, 80, 85, 90, 91, 92, 93, 95, 99, 105, 110, 122, 136, 138, 143, 144, 147, 150, 155
"RIDE ON ALONE," 161
RIDE TO LEXINGTON, THE, 161
RIDES TO RICHMOND, 136
"RIVER, PASSING OVER THE," 228
ROBERT ALWAYS GOOD, 25

ROBERT WANTS TO ENLIST, SON, 82
ROBERT ENTERS ARMY, SON, 91
Rockbridge, Virginia, 223, 234
Rockbridge Baths, Virginia, 158
Rockbridge Bible Society, 218, 219, 222
"Rock of Ages," 214
Roman Brutus, 131
ROYAL SOUL WITHIN A ROYAL BODY, A, 242
RULER OF UNIVERSE, 82

S

SABBATH, NO, 85
SABBATH OBSERVANCE, ORDER FOR, 94; interview on, 126
SABBATH OBSERVANCE, ANOTHER ORDER FOR, 128
SACRIFICE HIS MEN, WILL NOT, 152
Saint George's Chapel, 22
Saint Louis, Missouri, 35, 36
Saint Paul's Church, Baltimore, Maryland, 197
Saint Paul's Church, Richmond, Virginia, 155, 157
Saint Peter's Church, Baltimore, Maryland, 42
Saint Peter's Church, New Kent, Virginia, 209
Saint Thomas Church, New York City, 164
Salary, 122
"SALUTE THE CHURCH OF GOD," 95
San Antonio, Texas, 58
San Francisco, California, 193
Saunders, Herbert C., 191
Savannah, Georgia, 85, 88, 89, 210
Scott, General Winfield, 60, 61, 62, 66, 77

INDEX

Scott, Sir Walter, 22
Seaton, Miss Josephine, 197
SELF-DENIAL, 134
Sermon, baccalaureate, 171
SERMONS, LIKED PRACTICAL, 171
SERVICE IN BRIGADE, ATTENDS, 92
SERVICE UNDER THE TREES, DIVINE, 137
SEVEN DAYS' BATTLES, 93
Sewanee, Tennessee, 159
Sewell's Mountain, Camp on, 83, 84
Sharpsburg, Maryland, 95
"Shirley," Virginia, 210
SLANDER, REFUTES, 193
Slang, 204
SLAVERY, OPPOSED, 191
Slavery, views of, 50, 51, 58, 67, 75, 102, 191
SLAVES, FREES HIS, 100
SOCKS FOR SERVANTS, 84
SOLDIERS, LEE'S, 234
SON DECIDE FOR HIMSELF, 72
SON FITZHUGH WOUNDED, 109
SON FITZHUGH CAPTURED, 116
Son of man, stood on the Mount, 67
SORROW, COMFORT IN, 199
South Carolina, 85
Southern Baptist Theological Seminary, 172
Southern Collegian, 228
SOUTHERN HISTORIAN, 247
SPECIAL SINS, 214
SPEECH, CLEAN IN, 204
Spottsylvania Court House, 137
Springfield, Illinois, Lincoln at, 72
Stephens, Alexander H., vice-president of Confederacy, 68; description of Lee, 68, 233

STEPHENS, ALEXANDER H., 238
Stewart, Rev. Henry Johns, 107
Stiles, Major, 215
"Stratford," Virginia, birthplace of Lee, 23; daughters visit, 85
STUART, DEATH OF GENERAL, 136
Stuart, Miss Margaret, 130
SUBLIME HEIGHTS, 251
SUFFERED ENOUGH, NOT, 89
SUNDAY SCHOOL SCHOLAR, NEW, 178
SUNDAY TRAVELING, NO, 177
SUNSET, TOWARD THE, 208
SUPERINTENDENT OF WEST POINT, 45
SURRENDER, DECISION TO, 151
SUSTAINED BY DIVINE PROVIDENCE, 53
SYMPATHY FOR SOLDIERS, 121

T

TABLE, BLESSING AT THE, 145
Taskmaster's eye, 30
TAXES, PAYING, 115
Temperance, 32
TEMPERANCE, FRIENDS OF, 200
TEMPER, LOSING HIS, 203, 204
TESTIMONIAL, 219
Texas, Camp Brown, 50, 52
Texas, Camp Cooper, 50, 53, 54
Texas, Department of, 58
Texas, Fort Mason, 52, 59
TEXAS, GOES TO, 49
THANKFUL FOR PRAYERS, 143
Thayer, Colonel, 33
TOBACCO, 203
Tobacco, avoided, 32; Fitzhugh, 57

299

INDEX

TOWARD THE SUNSET, 208
Tractarian movement, 37
TRACTS AND PRAYER BOOKS, 141
"Traveller," General Lee's war horse, 136, 142, 148, 161, 279
TRUSTEES, REFUSES OFFERS FROM BOARD OF, 189
TRUSTEES, REPORT TO BOARD OF, 180

U

UNITED STATES ARMY, OFFERED COMMAND OF, 65
United States Grand Jury, 155
University of the South, 159
UNPUBLISHED LETTER, 70
UPPER ROOM, THE, 60

V

Valentine, Edward V., 215, 242
Valley Mountain, Camp, 79, 80, 81, 82
Valley of Humiliation, 152
Vestry, 37, 225
VICTORIES, GIVER OF ALL, 88
VICTORY, GIVER OF ALL, 98
VICTORY, ONLY GIVER OF, 104
VICTORY SERVICE, 228
Virginia Bible Society, 194
VIRGINIA BIBLE SOCIETY, 224
VIRGINIA, CASTS LOT WITH, 64
Virginia Convention, 65
VIRGINIA FORCES, TAKES COMMAND OF, 65
VIRGINIA, GOVERNOR OF, 65, 66
Virginia joined Confederate States, 69
Virginia Military Institute, 206
Virtue, equal to calamity, 153

VIRTUE, PURITY AND, 57
VISCOUNT WOLSELEY, 248
VISITS DAUGHTER'S GRAVE, 210
VISITS FATHER'S GRAVE, 87
VISITS MOTHER'S GIRLHOOD HOME, 210

W

Walker, the Rev. Cornelius, Lee's letter, 71
War, cruel, 99
WAR INEVITABLE, 69
WASHINGTON, AGAIN REFERRED TO COLONEL, 83
Washington, City of, 56, 59, 61, 65
WASHINGTON, DEATH OF COLONEL, 83
Washington, George, 23, 24, 28, 34, 61, 65, 83, 90, 122, 206, 209, 235, 278, 280, 281
Washington the Christian, George, 13
Washington, Mrs., 34, 55, 61, 281
Washington, Life of, Everett's, 59
Washington, Recollections of George, 78
WASHINGTON COLLEGE, ELECTED PRESIDENT, 159
WASHINGTON COLLEGE FACULTY, 236
Washington and Lee University, address before, 153
WEDDING, ANNIVERSARY OF, 138
WELFARE OF MEN, INTEREST IN, 134
WEST POINT, AT, 32
West Point Military Academy, about to leave for, 29; preparation for, 31; entered, 32; son Custis at, 43; superintendent, 45

INDEX

West Point, Superintendent of, 45
Whipple, Visit of Bishop, 199
Whisky, 56, 201
"White House," Virginia, Fitzhugh's home, 84; Mrs. Lee there, 90; burned, 92, 122, 209
White Sulphur Springs, North Carolina, 97, 158, 190, 209, 210
White, John S., 222
White, William G., 222
White, the Rev. Dr. W. S., 162, 164, 229
"Widow Custis," 90
Wife Driven from Home, His, 70
Wife Leaves Arlington, 73
Wife, Letter to Sick, 52
Wife on Christmas Day, 1861, to, 86
Wife to Leave Home, Urges, 70
Willard Hotel, Lincoln at, 62

Williamsport, Virginia, 117
William the Conqueror, 21
Wilmer, Bishop Joseph P., 75, 159
Wilson, David J., 177
Winchester, Virginia, 85, 95
Windsor, 22
Wine, 201
Woodbridge, Rev. George, 224
Woodstock, 22
Word in Season, A, 213
World, A Glorious, 78
Wrong, Would Not Do What Is, 58

Y

Young Men's Christian Association, 177
Young Men's Christian Association, Honorary Member of, 178
Young Men's Christian Association, address, 172; report of trustees, 181; gifts to, 212, 239

RECOMMENDED FURTHER READING

If you liked this book, the editors of Mott Media suggest that you order one or more of the following biographies of famous Christians.

GEORGE WASHINGTON THE CHRISTIAN
George Washington was God's man of the hour. His military and political success was motivated by his consistent faith that God was controlling the majestic event of which he was a part. This book completes the profile of the man who was "First in the hearts of his countrymen."

ABRAHAM LINCOLN THE CHRISTIAN
This book answers the questions which have surrounded the sincerity of Lincoln's spiritual life. The author demonstrates that the president moved through several stages of religious activity until a family tragedy caused him to give his life to Christ.

FOR YOUNG READERS AGES 8-12

ISAAC NEWTON
John Tiner's biography of Isaac Newton fills a gap in our knowledge and understanding of the spiritual life of a man who is usually recognized only for his scientific achievements. His inventions have overshadowed his lifelong practice of Bible study and prayer.

For more information on the **above books: Write:**

MOTT MEDIA, P.O. Box 236, MILFORD, MI 48042

NAME _____

ADDRESS _____

CITY _____ STATE _____ ZIP _____

SELECTION(S) _____

_____